IN THE RAYS OF LIGHT

LIVING THE QURAN
THROUGH
THE LIVING QURAN

SŪRAH AL-FĀTIḤA

THE OPENING

Written by Shaykh Muḥsin Qarā'atī
Translated by Saleem Bhimji

Edited by Arifa Hudda

ISBN 978-1-927930-63-2

Commentary of Sūrah al-Fātiḥa
A Translation from *Tafsīr-e Nūr*
Written by Shaykh Muḥsin Qarā'atī

Translated by Saleem Bhimji
Edited by Arifa Hudda

Published by Islamic Publishing House

www.iph.ca · iph@iph.ca

Cover Design and Layout by Saleem Bhimji

Contents

Foreword by the Translator i

An Introduction to Sūrah al-Fātiḥa 5
Merits of Recitation 10

Part I: In the Name of Allah – Verse 1 11
Thinking Points 11
The Features of this Phrase 18
The Status of the *Basmalah* 21
Analysis of the *Basmalah* 23
The Name "Allah" 26
General and Specific Mercy 27
Take Away Messages 30

Part II: Praise be to Allah – Verse 2 33
Thinking Points 33
Take Away Messages 43

Part III: A Compassionate Creator – Verse 3 45
Thinking Points 45
Take Away Messages 46

Part IV: Day of Judgement – Verse 4 47
Thinking Points 47
Take Away Messages 51

Part V: Complete Worship – Verse 5 53
Thinking Points 53
Take Away Messages 54

Part VI: The Straight Path – Verse 6 57
Thinking Points 57
Take Away Messages 67

Part VII: Deviation in Beliefs – Verse 7 69
Points 69
The Recipients of Wrath 71
The Misguided in the Quran 78

In the Name of Allah,
the All-Compassionate,
the All-Merciful

Foreword by the Translator

From the multitudes of commentaries *(tafāsīr)* that have been written by Muslim scholars over the past 12 centuries in their attempts to better understand the Quran and make it relevant to the lives of everyday Muslims, the present work of Shaykh Muḥsin Qarāʾatī, *Tafsīr-e Nūr* – The Exegesis of Light, is a unique attempt to bring the Quran into the homes of all of humanity.

Although sometimes very brief in his explanation, Shaykh Muḥsin makes up for the brevity of the commentary by providing the reader with **Take Away Messages**. These detailed points guide the readers to key pieces of guidance on how to make the Quran relevant to their daily lives – thus, being able to *Live the Quran Through the Living Quran.*

We hope and pray that the translation and publication of this commentary serves to bridge the great divide which has existed within the Muslim community for generations and allows them to benefit from the beautiful teachings of the Noble Quran in their daily lives.

The initial project to translate *Tafsīr-e Nūr* into English was envisioned in early 2018 and was initially meant to strictly be a podcast rendition of the translation.

However, due to popular demand and the support of well-wishers around the world, we expanded the scope of this project to release the PDF of the commentary of each chapter of the Quran as we completed them.

With the advancement in Print-On-Demand services globally, we have taken it a step further and decided to release the translation of the commentary of each chapter in print version.

Most commentaries of the Quran are published with each volume consisting of hundreds of pages, and this often puts some people off from wanting to try and understand the Quran. It is our hope that by publishing the commentary of the Quran in the format we have chosen – that is, chapter by chapter – readers will be encouraged to pick up the exegesis of the chapter that interests them the most. In this way, over time, they will have read the commentary of the entire Quran, gaining inspiration from its teachings.

As we present this work to our readers, we are deeply grateful to all of those who have made it possible.

We extend our heartfelt thanks to our editor, Sr. Arifa Hudda, whose tireless dedication and expertise have been instrumental in bringing this project to fruition. For almost 25 years, Sr. Arifa has been a cornerstone of the Islamic

Publishing House, guiding our publications with her keen insight and unwavering commitment to excellence. Her contribution to this work, as with all our publications, has been invaluable.

We would like to thank those donors who financially contributed towards the publishing of this book, as well as the other books in this series, and we ask you to recite a Sūrah al-Fātiḥa for their rewards and their dearly departed loved ones *(marhūmīn)*.

We are also profoundly grateful to our well-wishers, whose generous support – in many ways – enabled us to undertake this ambitious project. Their belief in the importance of the Quran, and their commitment to fostering a deeper understanding of the Book of Allah within our community have been a constant source of inspiration and encouragement.

In closing, if you would like to support this project by sponsoring its publication, either individually or with your family, friends, and community members, choose a chapter of the Quran that you would like to see published, and contact us at iph@iph.ca for more information.

In conclusion, we pray to Allah ﷻ to accept the translation of this brief, yet unique look into Sūrah al-Fātiḥa, and that we can spread the beautiful teachings of Allah ﷻ through *Living the Quran Through the Living Quran*.

Saleem Bhimji
Director *of the* Islamic Publishing House
25th of Muḥarram, 1447 AH

21st of July, 2025 CE
Kitchener, ON, Canada

سُورَةُ الفَاتِحَة

An Introduction to Sūrah al-Fātiḥa

Sūrah al-Fātiḥa, whose other name is Fātiḥa al-Kitāb, literally means "The Opening of the Book." It is also known as Sūrah al-Ḥamd, and it contains 7 verses.[1] It is the only chapter of the Quran which every Muslim is obligated to recite a minimum of ten times a day in their five obligatory daily prayers.[2] If the recitation of this chapter of the Quran is intentionally omitted, then one's prayers are rendered null and void, as the famous *ḥadīth* says: "There is no *ṣalāt* except with the [recitation] of the Opening of the Book."[3]

---

[1] The number seven plays a prominent role in Islam. In the Quran, it is noted that there are seven heavens; seven days in the week; the walking back and forth between the mountains of Ṣafā and Marwa in Mecca during the act of *saʿī* is seven; the number of *ṭawāfs* (circumambulations) around the Kaʿbah during the pilgrimages of *Ḥajj* and *ʿUmrah* are seven; there are seven stones which are thrown at the manifestations of the Devil in Mina (the act of *ramī)*, and many more instances.

[2] It is recited in the first and second *rakʿāt* of each of the five daily prayers. It should be noted that this chapter of the Quran must also be recited in the recommended prayers such as the daily *Nawāfil,* and other recommended prayers. (Tr.)

[3] Muḥaddith Nūrī, *Mustadrak al-Wasāʾil,* Vol. 4, Ḥadīth 4,365. The Arabic text of this is as follows:

لَا صَلَاةَ إِلَّا بِفَاتِحَةِ الْكِتَابِ.

According to a *ḥadīth* from the well-known companion, Jābir ibn ʿAbdullāh al-Anṣārī, Prophet Muḥammad ﷺ has been quoted as saying: "This is the best chapter of the Quran."

In addition, according to a *ḥadīth* which is narrated from Ibn ʿAbbās, Sūrah al-Ḥamd is the foundation of the Quran.

Further to this, it has been stated in a *ḥadīth* that: "If this chapter of the Quran were to be recited 70 times over a deceased person [with full conviction in the power of this chapter], then do not be surprised if that dead person comes back to life."[4]

From the naming of this chapter as *Fātiḥa al-Kitāb* – the Opening of the Book – which was done directly[5] by the Prophet ﷺ, all of the verses of the Quran were collected during the lifetime of the final Messenger of Allah ﷺ, and were available in a book form. As well, it was by his decree that this chapter was placed at the beginning of the Quran [even though it was not the first revelation given to Prophet Muḥammad ﷺ].

In the famous *Ḥadīth al-Thaqalayn*, on the two weighty things, the Prophet ﷺ has been quoted as saying: "I leave

---

[4] ʿAllāmah Majlisī, *Biḥār al-Anwār*, Vol. 92, Pg. 257. The Arabic text of this is as follows:

أَنَّهُ فِي الْفَاتِحَةِ وَأَنَّهَا لَوْ قُرِئَتْ عَلَى مَيِّتٍ سَبْعِينَ مَرَّةً ثُمَّ رُدَّتْ فِيهِ الرُّوحُ مَا كَانَ ذٰلِكَ عَجَبًا.

[5] Shaykh Ṣadūq, *ʿUyūn al-Akhbār al-Riḍā*, Vol. 2, Pg. 27.

behind you two weighty things – the Book of Allah and my family…"[6]

From this *ḥadīth,* it is also clear that the verses which Allah ﷻ sent down to Prophet Muḥammad ﷺ through Angel Jibrā'īl ؑ were collected in the form of a Book during the lifetime of the Prophet ﷺ, and it was known and widely recognized as "The Book of Allah" amongst the Muslims.

The verses of Sūrah al-Fātiḥa contain multiple topics, including:

1. Glimpses of Allah ﷻ and His Attributes.
2. The acceptance of the Rulership and Lordship of Allah ﷻ.
3. The Day of Judgement.
4. The recognition of and request to traverse upon the Path of the Truth.
5. Requesting to be able to follow on the Path of the Friends *(Awliyā')* of Allah ﷻ and showing devotion to them.
6. The declaration of disavowal of those who have gone astray, as well as those who have earned the anger and wrath of Allah ﷻ.

---

[6] *Biḥār al-Anwār,* Vol. 2, Pg. 100. The Arabic text of this is as follows:

إِنِّي تَارِكٌ فِيكُمُ الثَّقَلَيْنِ كِتَابَ اللهِ وَعِتْرَتِي...

Sūrah al-Ḥamd, just like the rest of the Quran, is a source of cure – both a cure for physical pains, and spiritual sicknesses.[7]

Before we delve into the commentary of Sūrah al-Ḥamd, by way of introducing this all-important chapter of the Quran, let us review some of the lessons in spiritual building which can be learnt from this chapter. Later in our discussion, we will review these in greater detail:

1. Through the recitation of Sūrah al-Ḥamd, specifically *Bismillāhir Raḥmānir Raḥīm* – 'In the Name of Allah, the All-Compassionate, the All-Merciful,' an individual cuts off their hopes from everyone and everything other than Allah ﷻ.
2. By saying the verse *Rabbil ʿĀlamīn* – 'The Lord of the Universe,' and *Māliki Yawmid Dīn* – 'Master of the Day of Judgement,' an individual begins to feel a sense of being maintained and owned by Allah ﷻ and can put aside all feelings of pride and arrogance.
3. Through the word *al-ʿĀlamīn* – 'the Universe,' a believer can establish a connection between oneself and everything in existence that Allah ﷻ has created.
4. Through the two Attributes of Allah ﷻ *al-Raḥmān, al-Raḥīm* – the All-Compassionate, the All-Merciful,' a believer places oneself under the shadow of the Grace of Allah ﷻ.
5. By saying *Māliki Yawmid Dīn* – 'Master of the Day of Judgement,' the heedlessness which one may feel in regard to the future is alleviated because a believer

---

[7] The late ʿAllāmah Aminī ؒ, in his commentary of Sūrah al-Fātiḥa, has narrated multiple traditions in these regards.

realizes that Allah ﷻ is the Ultimate Authority, and as such, there is no need for concern of any oppression or tyranny, as He will rule on that Day with complete justice and fairness.

6. By saying *Iyyāka naʿbudu* – 'You alone do we worship,' all forms of pride and attempts at boasting are destroyed.
7. By reciting *Iyyāka nastaʿīn* – 'You alone do we seek help (from),' we remove all fear in our hearts which may exist with regards to the so-called super-powers of the world.
8. From the word *anʿamta* – 'blessings,' we understand that all blessings lie in His hand.
9. By saying *Ihdināṣ Ṣirāṭal Mustaqīm* – 'Keep us on the Straight Path,' we seek to be guided onto the Straight Path by Allah ﷻ.
10. By reciting *Ṣirāṭal ladhīna ʿanamta ʿalayhim* – 'The Path of those whom You have showered your blessings upon,' we announce to the world that we are connected to those who are on the Path of the Truth.
11. By concluding and stating *Ghayril maghdhūbi ʿalayhim wa lā ḍhālīn* – 'Not the path of those who have earned Your anger, nor of those who have gone astray,' we seek to distance and declare our immunity from falsehood and the people of falsehood.

Merits of Recitation[8]

Regarding the virtue of this chapter, it has been narrated that Prophet Muḥammad ﷺ said: "Any Muslim who recites the Opening of the Book (Sūrah al-Fātiḥa) will be given a reward as if they recited two-thirds of the Quran, and as if they gave charity to every believing man and woman."[9]

According to another narration: "Any Muslim who recites Sūrah al-Fātiḥa will receive the reward of someone who recited the entire Quran, and it is as if they sent a gift to every believing man and woman."

The reference to two-thirds of the Quran may be because one part of the Quran focuses on Allah ﷻ, another part on the Day of Judgement, and another part on rules and commandments – and the first two parts are present in Sūrah al-Fātiḥa. In the second *ḥadīth* that mentions the rewards of reciting the entire Quran, it may be because from one perspective, all the Quran can be summarized as being about faith and action – both of which are combined in Sūrah al-Fātiḥa.

[8] Extracted from *Tafsīr-e Nemūnah* of Āyatullāh Nāṣir Makārim Shīrāzī.

[9] *Mustadrak al-Wasā'il*, Vol. 4, Pg. 331, Section 44, Ḥadīth 4,706. The Arabic text of this is as follows:

أَيُّمَا مُسْلِمٍ قَرَأَ فَاتِحَةَ الْكِتَابِ أُعْطِيَ مِنَ الْأَجْرِ كَأَنَّمَا قَرَأَ ثُلُثَيِ الْقُرْآنِ وَأُعْطِيَ مِنَ الْأَجْرِ كَأَنَّمَا تَصَدَّقَ عَلَىٰ كُلِّ مُؤْمِنٍ وَمُؤْمِنَةٍ.

Part I: In the Name of Allah – Verse 1

بِسۡمِ ٱللَّهِ ٱلرَّحۡمَٰنِ ٱلرَّحِيمِ

In the Name of Allah, the All-Compassionate, the All-Merciful.

Thinking Points

Among various groups and nations, it is customary that when they begin any important task which has any worth to it, they start by taking the name of one of their great, respected personalities whom they adore – looking for blessings and sanctification of their actions, with the hopes that their actions may reach fruition.

Of course, people act in this way based on either truthful or erroneous beliefs.

Sometimes, people may start an act in the name of the idols they worship; others may start by taking the name of their despotic rulers such as their heads of state. At other times, people may start with the Name of Allah ﷻ and the close friends *(Awliyā')* of Allah ﷻ just as took place in the Battle of Khandaq[10] in which the Messenger of Allah ﷺ

[10] The Battle of Khandaq (also known as the Battle of the Trench) took place in 627 CE (5 AH) near Medina. It was a pivotal confrontation between the Muslims – led by Prophet Muḥammad ﷺ – and a coalition of tribes of the Quraysh and their allies. After suffering losses at Badr and Uḥud, the Quraysh

threw down the first arrow after taking the Name of His Creator and Sustainer – Allah ﷻ.[11]

The phrase *Bismillāhir Raḥmānir Raḥīm* – 'I begin in the Name of Allah, the All-Compassionate, the All-Merciful' begins the Book of Allah ﷻ – the Quran. Not only is this phrase the start of this Heavenly Book, but rather, this phrase is at the beginning of all the Divinely sent Books which Allah ﷻ sent for the guidance of humanity.

This phrase also initiated the actions of past Prophets:

1. When the ark of Prophet Nūḥ ﷺ began to sail amongst the tumultuous waves of the great flood, Nūḥ ﷺ said to his companions 'Embark in it (upon the ark) in the Name of Allah...'[12] – meaning that the

---

sought to annihilate the Muslims by planning to besiege the city of Medina. Salmān al-Muḥammadī (better known as Salmān al-Fārisī), a companion of Persian origin, proposed digging a trench around the city to prevent enemy forces from advancing, a tactic unfamiliar to the Arabs. The Muslims, under the leadership of Prophet Muḥammad ﷺ, worked tirelessly to complete the trench in time. During the siege, the Quraysh and their allies faced frustration, as their cavalry was unable to cross the trench. In a climactic duel, Imam 'Alī ﷺ, known for his bravery and unwavering support of the Prophet ﷺ, defeated the Qurayshi champion 'Amrū ibn 'Abd Wudd, a key moment that demoralized the enemy forces. The siege ultimately failed due to the Muslims' defenses. This victory solidified the Muslims' position in Arabia, and demonstrated the significance of faith, unity, and strategic planning in overcoming adversity.

[11] *Biḥār al-Anwār*, Vol. 20, Pg. 218.

[12] Quran, Sūrah Hūd (11), Verse 41:

﴿وَقَالَ ٱرْكَبُوا۟ فِيهَا بِسْمِ ٱللَّهِ...﴾

setting sail and the stopping of this ark will be done in the Name of Allah ﷻ.

2. When Prophet Sulaymān ؑ invited the Queen of Sabā (Sheeba) to believe in the teachings given to him by Allah ﷻ, he began his invitation letter with this same phrase of *Bismillāhir Raḥmānir Raḥīm.*[13]

Imam ʿAlī ؑ mentioned how this phrase is the source of blessings in one's actions, and to disregard it will lead to failure. In addition, the Commander of the Faithful ʿAlī ؑ told an individual who was writing the phrase 'In the Name of Allah…' that he needs to ensure that he: 'Write it in beautiful writing.'[14]

We have been advised to verbally utter the phrase *Bismillāhir Raḥmānir Raḥīm* – 'In the Name of Allah, the All-Compassionate, the All-Merciful' throughout our days: before we begin any task; during the times of eating, sleeping, or writing something; when getting into our ride – whether this be an animal or a vehicle; when we go on any journey; and many other times in our day-to-day lives.

The emphasis on using this phrase is so much that if an animal is slaughtered without taking the Name of Allah ﷻ, then it is forbidden *(ḥarām)* for the meat of it to be consumed. The mystery behind this ruling is that even the food which a person consumes must be purposeful and have a Divine direction and goal which is achieved through the saying of this phrase.

---

[13] Quran, Sūrah al-Naml (27), Verse 30:

﴿إِنَّهُۥ مِن سُلَيۡمَٰنَ وَإِنَّهُۥ بِسۡمِ ٱللَّهِ ٱلرَّحۡمَٰنِ ٱلرَّحِيمِ ٣٠﴾

[14] Muttaqī Hindī, *Kanz al-ʿUmmāl*, Ḥadīth 29,558.

We also read in the *aḥādīth* that we must never forget the phrase 'In the Name of Allah…' even if we are writing a line of poetry.

Lastly, there are *aḥādīth* in which the benefits for a person who teaches a child to recite the phrase *Bismillāhir Raḥmānir Raḥīm* – 'In the Name of Allah, the All-Compassionate, the All-Merciful' for the first time have been clearly stated, and the rewards mentioned in those traditions are not something trivial.[15]

Having said all of this, a question may come into our mind: Why have we been encouraged to start every task with the phrase *Bismillāhir Raḥmānir Raḥīm* – 'In the Name of Allah, the All-Compassionate, the All-Merciful?'

The answer to this question is that this phrase is a symbol and slogan of the Muslims, and every action which a Muslim performs must take on the 'Colour of Allah ﷻ.'[16]

---

[15] Baḥrānī, Syed Hāshim, *Tafsīr al-Burhān*, Vol. 1, Pg. 43.

[16] The phrase "Colour of Allah" originates from the Quran, specifically in Sūrah al-Baqarah (2), Verse 138 where Allah ﷻ says:

﴿صِبْغَةَ ٱللَّهِ وَمَنْ أَحْسَنُ مِنَ ٱللَّهِ صِبْغَةً وَنَحْنُ لَهُۥ عَـٰبِدُونَ ١٣٨﴾

"[Take on] the Colour of Allah. And who is better than Allah in [imparting] Colour? And we are His worshippers."

The meaning of "Colour of Allah" is that the term *"ṣibghah"* in Arabic literally translates to "dye" or "colour." Metaphorically, it signifies the Divine Imprint, Nature, or Essence imparted by Allah ﷻ. This concept is understood as adopting the Attributes, Values, and Guidance of Allah ﷻ into one's life.

Spiritual Transformation: Just as dye changes the colour of a fabric, being "coloured" by Allah ﷻ refers to the transformative

When we look at the world around us, we see how a particular company will, in one factory, produce various products. They will ensure that their logo and insignia are emblazoned on the product and its packaging – whether it be an individual product, or multiple products packaged together. For example, a factory which produces Chinaware – things like plates, cups, bowls, etc. – will ensure that their logo is placed on each dish that they make – whether they are large dishes or small ones.

Another example is that of the flag of a country. It will normally be seen flying in front of government offices, schools, and military bases of that country; it will also be perched on boats and ships which are registered to that country; and lastly, the flag may also be prominently displayed on the desks of government employees.

---

effect of living in accordance with His Divine teachings. It reflects becoming immersed in faith, and embodying qualities such as mercy, justice, and kindness.

Faith and Identity: It signifies the identity and worldview shaped by Islam, where a believer's actions and character align with Divine Will, distinguishing them as worshippers of Allah ﷻ.

Submission and Devotion: It also highlights the idea that the Guidance of Allah ﷻ is the most beautiful and perfect "dye," better than any human construct or ideology, and that true worship lies in embodying His Path.

Thus, the "Colour of Allah" symbolizes living a life infused with the attributes, teachings, and moral framework provided by Allah ﷻ, making faith a defining aspect of a believer's identity. (Tr.)

Thus, this phrase of *Bismillāhir Raḥmānir Raḥīm* is the sign or flag of Islam and Muslims.

Another question which comes up is that is this phrase *Bismillāhir Raḥmānir Raḥīm* – 'In the Name of Allah, the All-Compassionate, the All-Merciful' – an independent verse *(āyah)* of the Quran?

The answer to this question is: According to the beliefs of the immaculate family of the Prophet of Allah ﷺ – the Ahlul Bayt ؑ – who have a one-hundred year precedent over all of the other religious leaders of the various Jurisprudential Schools *(Madhāhib)*, and who sacrificed their lives in the way of Allah ﷻ, and whose immaculate character is testified directly by the Quran (see Sūrah al-Aḥzāb (33), the last portion of Verse 33) – we are taught that it is indeed an independent verse and a part of the Quran – not something that has come from outside and has been introduced into the Word of Allah ﷻ.

In his famous exegesis, the Sunnī commentator of the Quran, Fakhr al-Dīn al-Rāzī, provides thirteen proofs for why this phrase is a part of the actual chapter of the Quran.

In addition, another Sunnī commentator, al-Ālūsī also shares this same belief.

It is mentioned in the *Musnad* of Aḥmad ibn Ḥanbal that this phrase is part of the chapter of Sūrah al-Fātiḥa.[17]

There are some Muslims who do not consider this phrase to be a part of each chapter of the Quran; thus, they do not recite it in their daily prayers before beginning the second chapter of the Quran; however, such people have been

---

[17] *Musnad* of Aḥmad ibn Ḥanbal, Vol. 3, Pg. 177, and Vol. 4, Pg. 85.

reprimanded throughout the history of Islam. For example, in the *Mustadrak* of al-Ḥākim it is mentioned that: "One day when Muʿāwiyah [ibn Abū Sufyān] was reciting his *ṣalāt*, he did not recite the phrase: 'In the Name of Allah, the All-Compassionate, the All-Merciful.' The people protested this action of his and rebuked him: 'Did you steal or forget [this verse of the Quran]?'"[18]

The immaculate Imams of the Ahlul Bayt ﷺ insisted that this phrase must be recited in an articulated voice – not whispered – in the *ṣalāt*.[19]

There is an event that is recorded as having taken place in the history of Islam and the Muslims, in which an individual who did not recite the phrase 'In the Name of Allah, the All-Compassionate, the All-Merciful,' or did not consider it a part of the chapter of the Quran, was told by the 5th Imam, Muḥammad al-Bāqir ؑ: "They have stolen the most noble verse [of the Quran]."[20]

In the *Sunan* of the Sunnī scholar, al-Bayhaqī, a tradition has been reported which questions why there are some people who do not consider the phrase 'In the Name of Allah, the All-Compassionate, the All-Merciful' as being a part of each chapter of the Quran.[21]

---

[18] *Mustadrak al-Wasā'il*, Vol. 3, Pg. 233.

[19] Note that from the Jurisprudential perspective, there is a difference in this ruling between men and women. Please refer to the Islamic Laws manual of the *marjaʿ taqlīd* that you follow for more information.

[20] *Biḥār al-Anwār*, Vol. 85, Pg. 20.

[21] *Sunan* of al-Bayhaqī, Vol. 2, Pg. 50.

In his commentary on Sūrah al-Ḥamd, the late Shahīd Murtaḍā Muṭahharī mentions that individuals such as Ibn ʿAbbās, ʿĀṣim, Kasāʾī, Ibn ʿUmar, Ibn Zubayr, ʿAṭāʾ, and Ibn Ṭāwūs; as well as Sunnī scholars, such as Fakhr al-Dīn al-Rāzī, and al-Suyūṭī as being some of the many who considered the phrase 'In the Name of Allah, the All-Compassionate, the All-Merciful' as being part of Sūrah al-Fātiḥa – contrary to the beliefs of other companions and scholars of Islam – more specifically Sunnī scholars.

In his commentary of the Quran, the Sunnī scholar, al-Qurṭubī narrates a *ḥadīth* from Imam Jaʿfar al-Ṣādiq, in which he is quoted to have said that: "(The phrase) 'In the Name of Allah, the All-Compassionate, the All-Merciful,' is the crown of the chapters of the Quran, and it is only Sūrah al-Barāʾat (al-Tawbah) in which this [phrase] does not occur."

He goes on to note that this is according to the statement of Imam ʿAlī where he mentioned that 'In the Name of Allah, the All-Compassionate, the All-Merciful' is associated with safety and mercy, and the proclamation mentioned at the outset of Sūrah al-Tawbah is disavowal towards the disbelievers and polytheists, and this is not something congruent with love and mercy.[22]

The Features of this Phrase

In the phrase 'In the Name of Allah, the All-Compassionate,' the All-Merciful is:

---

[22] Shaykh Ṭabrisī, *Tafsīr Majmaʿ al-Bayān*; and *Tafsīr al-Kabīr* of Fakhr al-Dīn al-Rāzī.

1. A sign of the Colour and Dye of the Divine, and an expression of our belief in Monotheism *(Tawḥīd).*[23]
2. A token of Monotheism *(Tawḥīd).* Mentioning the name of anything or anyone other than Him is disbelief, and placing His Name alongside the name of anyone or anything else is an indicator of polytheism. We must never take any other name besides Allah ﷻ – neither alongside His Name, nor in its place.[24]
3. The secret to perpetuity, since whatever does not take on the Colour of Allah ﷻ is condemned to extinction.[25]
4. The goal to true love of Allah ﷻ, and complete trust and reliance in Him *(tawakkul).* We show our love

---

[23] Ḥuwayzī, ʿAbd ʿAlī, *Tafsīr Nūr al-Thaqalayn.*

[24] Not only is the Sacred Essence of Allah ﷻ free from all forms of polytheism, but also His Name is also one which is free from association with others, as the Quran says: 'Glorify the Name of Your Lord, the Highest' – 'سَبِّحِ اسْمَ رَبِّكَ الْأَعْلَى.' In addition, it is not permissible to start our actions by saying something like: "I start my actions in the Name of Allah and [the Prophet] Muḥammad ﷺ]. See *Ithbāt al-Huḍa* by Shaykh Ḥurr ʿĀmilī, Vol. 7, Pg. 482.

[25] Quran, Sūrah al-Qaṣaṣ (28), Verse 88:

﴿وَلَا تَدْعُ مَعَ ٱللَّهِ إِلَـٰهًا ءَاخَرَ لَآ إِلَـٰهَ إِلَّا هُوَ كُلُّ شَىْءٍ هَالِكٌ إِلَّا وَجْهَهُۥ لَهُ ٱلْحُكْمُ وَإِلَيْهِ تُرْجَعُونَ ۝٨٨﴾

"Do not call upon another god along with Allah. There is no god but He. Everything is perishable (and so perishing) except His 'Face' (His eternal Self and what is done in seeking His good pleasure). His alone is judgement and authority, and to Him you are being brought back."

to the One who is All-Compassionate *(al-Raḥmān)* and All-Merciful *(al-Raḥīm).* As such, we start all our actions with full trust in Him. It is through starting in His Name that we will be able to attract His Mercy.

5. The means to the eradication of pride, and the ability to manifest our inability in His Presence – realizing that only He can assist us.
6. The first step in true servitude *('Ubudiyyah).*
7. The source for Satan to distance himself from us. That person who is with Allah ﷻ will find that Satan will not be able to have any influence upon them.
8. The force through which a person will find success in their endeavours and will be able to protect all of their acts.
9. The remembrance of Allah ﷻ – meaning that by this, we are stating that 'O Allah, I have not forgotten You, and I never will!'
10. The way to describe our intentions – meaning that when we state this phrase, we are saying that 'O Allah, You are my goal – not the people, not the despots, not fame or glory, nor my lower desires.'
11. Imam 'Alī ibn Mūsā al-Riḍā ﷺ said that "The phrase 'In the Name of Allah, the All-Compassionate, the All-Merciful' is closer to the 'Greatest Name of Allah' (*al-Ism al-A'ẓam*) than the pupil of the eye is to the sclera (white part of the eye) which surrounds it."[26]

---

[26] Rafsanjānī, Akbar Hashemi, *Tafsīr Rahnamā.*

The Status of the *Basmalah*[27]

In a tradition narrated from Imam Ḥasan ibn ʿAlī al-ʿAskarī ﷺ, the 11th Imam, he regards the recitation of the *basmalah* as a sign of a believer, and that they should recite it in a pronounced voice, as opposed to a quiet whisper, in each of the daily prayers.[28]

Based on such traditions, we see that there is no difference of opinion among the Shīʿa scholars that the *basmalah* is a part of Sūrah al-Ḥamd, as well as a part of every other chapter of the Quran – other than chapter nine which is Sūrah at-Tawbah – and so when this or any other chapter of the Quran is recited in the daily prayers, a believer is obligated to say this phrase before reciting the Sūrah.[29]

---

[27] This section has been extracted from *The Clear Guidance* (Volume 1) published by Al-Kisa Foundation.
Basmalah is the phrase: In the Name of Allah, the All-Compassionate, the All-Merciful:

بِسۡمِ ٱللَّهِ ٱلرَّحۡمَٰنِ ٱلرَّحِيمِ

[28] *Wasāʾil al-Shīʿah*, Vol. 14, Pg. 478, Ḥadīth 19643. The initial portion of this tradition is as follows:

عَلَامَاتُ ٱلْمُؤْمِنِ خَمْسٌ صَلَاةُ ٱلْخَمْسِينَ وَ...

[29] In regard to the *basmalah* and its place in the daily *ṣalāh*, the religious jurists *(marājiʿ taqlīd)* have stated that it is recommended for men to recite this with a pronounced and loud voice (as opposed to an audible whisper) in all the daily prayers, in the first and second *rakʿat*. This opinion is shared by the late Āyatullāhs: Sayyid Ruḥullāh Khomeini, Shaykh Muḥammad

The fact that the *basmalah* is written before every *sūrah* of the printed Quran around the world proves that it is a part of each chapter, except for chapter nine, otherwise why would Muslims over the past 1,400 years have been writing it in the Quran?

In addition, whenever Muslims begin to recite the Noble Quran – even if they start mid-way in a chapter, they start with the *basmalah.*

With all of the emphasis which has been given by Prophet Muḥammad ﷺ and the Muslims on the importance of the *basmalah*, it is of no surprise that in the early days of Islamic history, the Muslims were quick to challenge anyone who dared to remove this verse from its well-established application.

During his period of governance, Muʿāwiyah ibn Abū Sufyān once led the congregational prayers, but he did not start his recitation of the Quran within the *ṣalāh* with the *basmalah.* This provoked anger and protests from the *muhājirīn* and the *anṣār* who were present. They objected to Muʿāwiyah and said to him: "Have you taken something away (which is not your property – meaning the *basmalah*),

---

Taqī Behjat, Sayyid Muḥammad Riḍā Gulpāygānī, and Shaykh Luṭfullāh Ṣāfī Gulpāygānī; and also the contemporary living Āyatullāhs, namely: Sayyid Sīstānī, Sayyid Khamenei, Shaykh Nāṣir Makārim Shīrāzī, and Sayyid Shubayrī Zanjānī. Women may recite this verse in a pronounced voice as well, if there are no non-related men *(non-maḥram)* in their vicinity, but if there are any men, then they must recite the *basmalah* in an audible whisper, not in a loud voice.

or did you forgot (because you did not start the recitation of the Quran in the prayers with the *basmalah*?!)"[30]

Analysis of the *Basmalah*

It is standard practice around the world that anytime people want to start something, they begin in a unique way. When it comes to sporting events, the national anthem of both teams' countries will be played; however, in the corporate world, directors of the company may initiate their annual employee meetings by reminding the staff about the company ethos, motto, etc.

When starting the Noble Quran, a book which is meant to be the blueprint of life for all of humanity from the time of its revelation until the end of time, it only makes sense for it to start in the Name of The One who Himself is Eternal – He who has been here since before time existed, and will continue to be after time comes to a halt – and that is none other than Allah ﷻ.

Therefore, Allah ﷻ begins His Book in His Name.

This is not a mere formality on His part, nor is it something which Muslims are meant to adhere to only when reading this Book, but rather, we are encouraged to energize our entire life with this phrase and to understand and imbibe its deeper meanings – if we wish to be successful in everything that we do.

---

[30] Bayhaqī, Vol. 2, Pg. 49; *Mustadrak* of Ḥākim al-Naysabūrī, Vol. 1, Pg. 233 – he related this event and mentioned that it is *ṣaḥīḥ*.

It is for this reason that Prophet Muḥammad ﷺ said: "Every important action which a person embarks upon that is not initiated in the Name of Allah will remain fruitless."[31]

In this and many other traditions, the phrase "will remain fruitless" has been used for various acts.

Some may read such traditions and have a perception that they performed certain actions without saying the *basmalah,* but yet they reached what they felt was the 'full potential' of that action. They do not feel or think that what they did was fruitless or without accomplishment.

However, we need to appreciate that the real fruit of an action is one in which the results are not limited to this temporal world; rather we must realize that actions done 'in the Name of Allah ﷻ' are eternal, and when we have that connection to Allah ﷻ by not only verbally 'saying' the *basmalah*, but dedicating our actions to Him, then we will see that in return, Allah ﷻ will reward us – not only in the limited span of the actions in this world, but even further than this – for eternity.

Due to the fact that we cannot see the rewards of the world to come, and we may not fully understand that there is another world after this in which the true manifestation of our deeds will be shown to us, we feel that our actions are visibly effective and successful even if we did not start them with the phrase, 'in the Name of Allah ﷻ.'

---

[31] *Biḥār al-Anwār*, Vol. 73, Pg. 305, Ḥadīth 1. The initial portion of this tradition is as follows:

كُلُّ أَمْرٍ ذِي بَالٍ لَمْ يُذْكَرْ...

In summary, our actions will be successful and endure when they are intertwined with the Eternal – meaning Allah ﷻ – and thus, when we start anything in His Name, we seek to multiply our rewards and efforts with His help and assistance.

Beginning in the Name of Allah ﷻ is so important that we see the previous Prophets of Allah ﷻ relied on Him through this phrase.

For example, when Prophet Nūḥ ﷺ was about to embark on his ark and sail away in safety from the flood which ended up destroying the remorseless people of his society, he began in the Name of Allah ﷻ. The Quran depicts this beautifully: "And Nūḥ said: 'Board it (the ark) in Allah's Name be its course and its anchorage. Surely my Lord is All-Forgiving, All-Merciful.'"[32]

In addition, when Prophet Sulaymān ﷺ wrote his historic letter inviting the Queen of Sabā to accept Islam, he too started in the Name of Allah ﷻ: "Indeed it (this letter) is from Sulaymān, and it is: 'In the Name of Allah, the All-Compassionate, the All-Merciful.'"[33]

It is in this same light that we see that other than chapter nine of the Quran – which was a declaration of confrontation against the deceitful, oppressive polytheists of Mecca to whom an ultimatum was given due to their

---

[32] Quran, Sūrah Hūd (11), Verse 41:

﴿وَقَالَ ارْكَبُوا فِيهَا بِسْمِ ٱللَّهِ مَجْرَاهَا وَمُرْسَاهَا إِنَّ رَبِّي لَغَفُورٌ رَحِيمٌ﴾

[33] Quran, Sūrah al-Naml (27), Verse 30:

﴿إِنَّهُ مِنْ سُلَيْمَانَ وَإِنَّهُ بِسْمِ ٱللَّهِ ٱلرَّحْمَٰنِ ٱلرَّحِيمِ﴾

incessant attacks against innocent people, all of the other chapters of the Quran begin with this great phrase.

The Name "Allah"

When we study the titles which Allah ﷻ has mentioned for Himself in the Quran, we see that each one relates to a specific quality which Allah ﷻ possesses, such as His Mercy, Compassion, Granting of Sustenance, Wisdom, etc.

However, the only name which is inclusive of all the titles that He possesses is "Allah;" and it is for this reason that we say that the other titles such as *al-Raḥmān*, *al-Ḥakīm*, *al-ʿAlīm*, etc. are all characteristics for His Name, Allah ﷻ. In other words, within the name Allah ﷻ are all the qualities and characteristics of Beauty *(Jamāl)* and Majesty *(Jalāl)*.

For example, Allah ﷻ says in the Quran: "Then indeed Allah is All-Forgiving *(Ghafūr)*, All-Merciful *(Raḥīm)*."[34]

In the verse which immediately follows this one, He says: "Then surely Allah is Hearing *(Samīʿ)*, Knowing *(ʿAlīm)*."[35]

Even though the Name Allah combines all of the qualities and traits inclusively, yet in a beautiful verse of the Quran, Allah ﷻ goes on to describes Himself by specifically signaling out eight of His qualities where He

---

[34] Quran, Sūrah al-Baqarah (2), Verse 226:

...﴿فَإِنَّ ٱللَّهَ غَفُورٌ رَّحِيمٌ﴾

[35] Quran, Sūrah al-Baqarah (2), Verse 227:

...﴿فَإِنَّ ٱللَّهَ سَمِيعٌ عَلِيمٌ﴾

says: "He is Allah, save whom there is no god; the Sovereign, the Pure, the Peace, the Author of Safety and Security, the All-Watchful Guardian, the All-Glorious, the All-Compelling, and the One Who has exclusive right to all greatness. All-Glorified is Allah in that He is absolutely exalted above what they associate with Him."[36]

The final point to consider when we reflect on the importance of His Name being Allah ﷻ and its comprehensive nature, is that for a person to revert to Islam, the first portion of the phrase which they need to say is: "I bear witness that there is no god worthy of worship except for Allah." One cannot substitute any of His other names in place of Allah ﷻ and expect to come into the fold of Islam. When they say the above phrase and then attest to the finality of Prophet Muḥammad ﷺ, then they are confirming the fact that all of the perfect qualities are contained within the name Allah ﷻ, and that they recognize Him as having all of these perfect qualities.

General and Specific Mercy

If Allah ﷻ had started the chapters of the Quran with a phrase like 'In the Name of Allah,' this would have been sufficient because as we said, His Name Allah covers all His Attributes.

---

[36] Quran, Sūrah al-Ḥashr (59), Verse 23:

﴿هُوَ ٱللَّهُ ٱلَّذِى لَآ إِلَٰهَ إِلَّا هُوَ ٱلْمَلِكُ ٱلْقُدُّوسُ ٱلسَّلَٰمُ ٱلْمُؤْمِنُ ٱلْمُهَيْمِنُ ٱلْعَزِيزُ ٱلْجَبَّارُ ٱلْمُتَكَبِّرُ ۚ سُبْحَٰنَ ٱللَّهِ عَمَّا يُشْرِكُونَ ٢٣﴾

However, Allah ﷻ has chosen to introduce Himself to His creations through two more qualities which are two variations of His Kindness and Generosity. We can say that out of all His qualities, these two are more appealing to the creations, and allow them to have a stronger bond with Him because they are addressing His Mercy and Compassion, rather than other things like His Power or Wrath.

The two traits of Allah ﷻ which are contained in the *basmalah, al-Raḥmān* and *al-Raḥīm*, both come from the same Arabic root of *raḥma* – mercy; however, they are manifested at different levels, and for varying times and circumstances.

This mercy is such that it is a place of refuge when there is chaos and unrest all around.

When a person turns to the One who is *al-Raḥmān* and *al-Raḥīm*, they are in fact turning to the place where they can find peace, refuge, solace, and comfort – just like when a person comes across the wild rapids of a violent river which eventually makes its way through the valley of a mountain only to wind up at a tranquil resting place.

Commentators of the Quran believe that *al-Raḥmān* points to the general Mercy of Allah ﷻ which embraces everything and everyone – Muslim and non-Muslim alike, good doers and sinners; while the trait of *al-Raḥīm* is a specific mercy which covers only the true, righteous, and devoted believers – and that too more so in the world to come.

Therefore, when the Quran uses the trait of *al-Raḥmān*, it normally does so in a very general treatment; however, when it uses *al-Raḥīm*, it tends to attach qualifiers to it to show that it is a specific form of mercy, such as when Allah ﷻ says: "...And He is All-Merciful towards the believers."[37]

There is a tradition from Imam Jaʿfar al-Ṣādiq (ʿa) in which he said: "Allah is that entity which all worship. In relation to all His creations - He is *al-Raḥmān*; while regarding the true believers - He is *al-Raḥīm*."[38]

Why not use Other Traits?

Out of the thousands of qualities and characteristics which Allah ﷻ has, why is it that in the 114 occurrences[39] of the *basmalah* in the Quran, He only used *al-Raḥmān* and *al-Raḥīm*? Why did the Almighty not use a variety of names to begin each chapter?

The answer to this question is that it is important to seek assistance through those qualities and characteristics which embrace all of the world of creation; names which everything in the universe can benefit from; attributes which those who are in times of difficulty can latch themselves onto – and out of the countless traits which

---

[37] Quran, Sūrah al-Aḥzāb (33), Verse 43:

﴿...وَكَانَ بِٱلْمُؤْمِنِينَ رَحِيمًا ﴿٤٣﴾﴾

[38] *Al-Kāfī*, Vol. 1, Pg. 114. The initial portion of this tradition is as follows:

وَٱللَّهُ إِلَهُ كُلِّ شَيْءٍ ٱلرَّحْمٰنُ بِجَمِيعِ خَلْقِهِ...

[39] This phrase initiates 113 of the 114 chapters of the Quran, while its 114th usage is found in Sūrah al-Naml (27), Verse 30 – in the letter that Prophet Sulaymān (ʿa) wrote to the Queen of Sabā:

﴿إِنَّهُۥ مِن سُلَيْمَٰنَ وَإِنَّهُۥ بِسْمِ ٱللَّهِ ٱلرَّحْمَٰنِ ٱلرَّحِيمِ﴾

Allah ﷻ has, the only ones that can really do this are these two qualities.

Allah ﷻ is clear about this in the Quran where He says: "...and My Mercy embraces all things..."[40]

Therefore, since Allah ﷻ bases His actions on mercy, and although consequences exist, they are the exception to the rule – and as believers, we must remember that the Mercy of Allah ﷻ takes precedence in our lives; and even in the contents of the Quran, and all of the do's and don'ts, there is also mercy contained in them.

Take Away Messages

1. The verse 'In the Name of Allah, the All-Compassionate, the All-Merciful' at the beginning of the *sūrahs* symbolize that the contents of the Quran have been revealed from the Source of Truth, and the Manifestation of Mercy.
2. The verse 'In the Name of Allah, the All-Compassionate, the All-Merciful' at the beginning of this Divinely-sent Book means that guidance is only achieved through seeking His assistance.
3. The verse 'In the Name of Allah, the All-Compassionate, the All-Merciful' is the phrase that both the speech of Allah ﷻ to people and people's speech to Allah ﷻ begins with.

---

[40] Quran, Sūrah al-Aʿrāf (7), Verse 156:

﴿...وَرَحْمَتِي وَسِعَتْ كُلَّ شَيْءٍ...﴾

4. Divine Mercy – like His Essence – is eternal and everlasting.
5. The expression of Divine Mercy in various forms indicates an emphasis on the concept of mercy.
6. Perhaps the placement of the words *al-Raḥmān* and *al-Raḥīm* at the beginning of this Book indicates that the Quran is a manifestation of Divine Mercy, just as the very act of creation and the sending of Prophets are manifestations of His Kindness and Mercy.

Part II: Praise be to Allah – Verse 2

ٱلْحَمْدُ لِلَّهِ رَبِّ ٱلْعَٰلَمِينَ ﴿٢﴾

"All praise (and gratitude) belongs to Allah (God) alone, the Lord of the Worlds."

Thinking Points

The word *'Rabb'* (Lord) refers to One who is both the Owner of something and plays a role in its growth and development. Knowing this, we can state that Allah ﷻ is our sole *Rabb* as He is both the true Owner of the Universe and everything within it, as well as its Director and Sustainer. Thus, all existence has an evolutionary movement and is guided along the path that Allah ﷻ has determined.

Besides Sūrah al-Ḥamd, four other chapters of the Quran, namely: al-Anʿām (6), al-Kahf (18), Sabaʾ (34), and Fāṭir (35) – also begin with the word *"Alḥamdulillāhi,"* but only in Sūrah al-Ḥamd is it followed by the phrase *"Rabb al-ʿĀlamīn"* (Lord of the Worlds).[41]

---

[41] These verses are:

﴿ٱلْحَمْدُ لِلَّهِ ٱلَّذِى خَلَقَ ٱلسَّمَٰوَٰتِ وَٱلْأَرْضَ وَجَعَلَ ٱلظُّلُمَٰتِ وَٱلنُّورَ ثُمَّ ٱلَّذِينَ كَفَرُوا۟ بِرَبِّهِمْ يَعْدِلُونَ ﴿١﴾﴾

"All praise (and gratitude) belongs to Allah, Who created the heavens and the Earth, and made the veils of darknesses and the

The concept of *'ḥamd'* (praise) combines both praise and gratitude. Human beings express praise in response to beauty, perfection, and elegance; and express gratitude in response to the blessings, service given to them, and kindness from others. Allah, the Exalted, deserves both praise for His perfection and beauty, and gratitude for His kindness and blessings.

---

light. Yet, those who disbelieve ascribe equals to their Lord." (Quran, Sūrah al-Anʿām (6), Verse 1)

﴿ٱلْحَمْدُ لِلَّهِ ٱلَّذِىٓ أَنزَلَ عَلَىٰ عَبْدِهِ ٱلْكِتَـٰبَ وَلَمْ يَجْعَل لَّهُۥ عِوَجَا ۝١﴾

"All praise (and gratitude) belongs to Allah, Who sent down on His servant (Prophet Muḥammad) the Book, and has not made any crookedness in it." (Quran, Sūrah al-Kahf (18), Verse 1)

﴿ٱلْحَمْدُ لِلَّهِ ٱلَّذِى لَهُۥ مَا فِى ٱلسَّمَـٰوَٰتِ وَمَا فِى ٱلْأَرْضِ وَلَهُ ٱلْحَمْدُ فِى ٱلْـَٔاخِرَةِ ۚ وَهُوَ ٱلْحَكِيمُ
ٱلْخَبِيرُ ۝١﴾

"All praise (and gratitude) belongs to Allah to Whom belongs whatever is in the heavens and whatever is on the Earth (for it is He Who created them and sustains them); and to Him belongs all praise in the Hereafter. And He is the All-Wise, the All-Aware." (Quran, Sūrah Saba' (34), Verse 1)

﴿ٱلْحَمْدُ لِلَّهِ فَاطِرِ ٱلسَّمَـٰوَٰتِ وَٱلْأَرْضِ جَاعِلِ ٱلْمَلَـٰٓئِكَةِ رُسُلًا أُو۟لِىٓ أَجْنِحَةٍ مَّثْنَىٰ وَثُلَـٰثَ
وَرُبَـٰعَ ۚ يَزِيدُ فِى ٱلْخَلْقِ مَا يَشَآءُ ۚ إِنَّ ٱللَّهَ عَلَىٰ كُلِّ شَىْءٍ قَدِيرٌ ۝١﴾

"All praise (and gratitude) belongs to Allah, the Originator of the heavens and the Earth (each with features and ordered principles), Who appoints the angels as messengers (conveying His commands) having wings, two, or three, or four, (or more). He increases in creation what He Wills. Surely, Allah has full Power over everything." (Quran, Sūrah Fāṭir (35), Verse 1)

The phrase *'Alḥamdulillāh'* is the best form of gratitude to Allah ﷻ. Whoever praises any perfection or beauty anywhere, in any language, is praising its Source. Of course, praising Allah ﷻ does not conflict with showing gratitude to creation, if it is in accordance with the command of Allah ﷻ and on His path.

We must always remember that Allah ﷻ is the Lord of all creation: "...And He is the Lord of everything...;"[42] and He is the Lord of whatever exists in the heavens and the Earth, and all that is between them: "He (Prophet Mūsā) said: 'Lord of the heavens and the Earth and whatever is between them...'"[43]

Imam ʿAlī ؑ says: "Of the inanimate objects and living beings – He is the Lord of both the living and the non-living. To Him belongs the creation and the command, blessed is Allah, Lord of the Worlds,"[44] – both creation and

---

[42] Quran, Sūrah al-Anʿām (6), Verse 164:

﴿...وَهُوَ رَبُّ كُلِّ شَيْءٍ... ﴾

[43] Quran, Sūrah al-Shuʿarāʾ (26), Verse 24:

﴿قَالَ رَبُّ ٱلسَّمَٰوَٰتِ وَٱلْأَرْضِ وَمَا بَيْنَهُمَآ... ﴾

[44] Shaykh Ṣadūq, *ʿIlal al-Sharāʾiʿ*, Vol. 2, Pg. 416, Section 157, Ḥadīth 3:

حَدَّثَنَا مُحَمَّدُ بْنُ الْقَاسِمِ الْأَسْتَرَآبَادِيُّ الْمُفَسِّرُ رَضِيَ اللَّهُ عَنْهُ قَالَ حَدَّثَنِي يُوسُفُ بْنُ مُحَمَّدِ بْنِ زِيَادٍ وَعَلِيُّ بْنُ مُحَمَّدِ بْنِ يَسَارٍ عَنْ أَبَوَيْهِمَا عَنِ الْحَسَنِ بْنِ عَلِيِّ بْنِ مُحَمَّدِ بْنِ عَلِيِّ بْنِ مُوسَى بْنِ جَعْفَرِ بْنِ مُحَمَّدِ بْنِ عَلِيِّ بْنِ الْحُسَيْنِ بْنِ عَلِيِّ بْنِ أَبِي طَالِبٍ عَلَيْهِ السَّلَامُ قَالَ:

Muḥammad ibn al-Qāsim al-Astarābādī, the commentator, may Allah be pleased with him, narrated to us: "Yūsuf ibn Muḥammad

---

ibn Ziyād, and ʿAlī ibn Muḥammad ibn Yasār narrated from their fathers, who narrated from Ḥasan ibn ʿAlī ibn Muḥammad ibn ʿAlī ibn Mūsā ibn Jaʿfar ibn Muḥammad ibn ʿAlī ibn Ḥusayn ibn ʿAlī ibn Abī Ṭālib (peace be upon him), who said:

جَاءَ رَجُلٌ إِلَى الرِّضَا عليه السلام فَقَالَ: يَا ابْنَ رَسُولِ اللّٰهِ: أَخْبِرْنِي عَنْ قَوْلِ اللّٰهِ عَزَّ وَجَلَّ أَلْحَمْدُ لِلّٰهِ رَبِّ الْعَالَمِينَ مَا تَفْسِيرُهُ.

'A man came to Imam al-Riḍā (peace be upon him) and said: 'O son of the Messenger of Allah, tell me about the meaning of Allah's words: 'All praise belongs to Allah, the Lord of the Worlds.' What does it mean?'

فَقَالَ لَقَدْ حَدَّثَنِي أَبِي عَنْ جَدِّي عَنِ الْبَاقِرِ عَنْ زَيْنِ الْعَابِدِينَ عَنْ أَبِيهِ عَلَيْهِ السَّلَامُ: أَنَّ رَجُلًا جَاءَ إِلَى أَمِيرِ الْمُؤْمِنِينَ عَلَيْهِ السَّلَامُ فَقَالَ: أَخْبِرْنِي عَنْ قَوْلِ اللّٰهِ عَزَّ وَجَلَّ أَلْحَمْدُ لِلّٰهِ رَبِّ الْعَالَمِينَ مَا تَفْسِيرُهُ؟

The Imam replied: 'My father narrated to me from my grandfather, who narrated from [Imam] al-Bāqir, who narrated from [Imam] Zayn al-ʿĀbidīn, who narrated from his father (peace be upon him), that a man came to the Commander of the Faithful (ʿAlī – peace be upon him) and said: 'Tell me about the meaning of the words of Allah, the Noble and Grand: 'All praise is due to Allah, the Lord of the Worlds.' What does it mean?''

فَقَالَ: أَلْحَمْدُ لِلّٰهِ هُوَ أَنْ عَرَّفَ عِبَادَهُ بَعْضَ نِعَمِهِ عَلَيْهِمْ جُمَلًا إِذْ لَا يَقْدِرُونَ عَلَى مَعْرِفَةِ جَمِيعِهَا بِالتَّفْصِيلِ لِأَنَّهَا أَكْثَرُ مِنْ أَنْ تُحْصَى أَوْ تُعْرَفَ فَقَالَ لَهُمْ قُولُوا أَلْحَمْدُ لِلّٰهِ عَلَى مَا أَنْعَمَ بِهِ عَلَيْنَا رَبِّ الْعَالَمِينَ.

He (Imām al-Riḍā, peace be upon him) replied: 'All praise belongs to Allah,' means that He made His servants aware of some of His blessings upon them in a general way, for they are incapable of knowing all of them in detail, as they are too numerous to count or fully comprehend. So, He told them to say: 'All praise belongs to Allah for what He has blessed us with, Lord of the Worlds.'

وَهُمُ الْجَمَاعَاتُ مِنْ كُلِّ مَخْلُوقٍ مِنَ الْجَمَادَاتِ وَالْحَيَوَانَاتِ أَمَّا الْحَيَوَانَاتُ فَهُوَ يَقْلِبُهَا فِي قُدْرَتِهِ وَيَغْذُوهَا مِنْ رِزْقِهِ وَيَحُوطُهَا بِكَنَفِهِ وَيُدَبِّرُ كُلًّا مِنْهَا بِمَصْلَحَتِهِ وَأَمَّا الْجَمَادَاتُ فَهُوَ يُمْسِكُهَا بِقُدْرَتِهِ يُمْسِكُ الْمُتَّصِلَ مِنْهَا أَنْ يَتَهَافَتَ وَيُمْسِكُ الْمُتَهَافِتَ مِنْهَا أَنْ يَتَلَاصَقَ وَيُمْسِكُ السَّمَاءَ أَنْ تَقَعَ عَلَى الْأَرْضِ إِلَّا بِإِذْنِهِ وَيُمْسِكُ الْأَرْضَ أَنْ تَنْخَسِفَ إِلَّا بِأَمْرِهِ إِنَّهُ بِعِبَادِهِ لَرَؤُفٌ رَحِيمٌ.

And ["The Worlds"] refers to all groups of creations - both inanimate and living beings. As for the living beings, He sustains them through His Power, provides them with sustenance, watches over them, and manages each of them in a way that benefits them. As for the inanimate beings, He holds them with His Power, preventing the connected from falling apart, and the scattered from merging together. He prevents the sky from collapsing upon the Earth except by His permission, and He keeps the Earth from sinking except by His command. Indeed, He is All-Kind and All-Merciful to His servants.

قَالَ عَلَيْهِ السَّلَامُ: رَبِّ الْعَالَمِينَ مَالِكِهِمْ وَخَالِقِهِمْ وَسَائِقِ أَرْزَاقِهِمْ إِلَيْهِمْ مِنْ حَيْثُ هُمْ يَعْلَمُونَ وَمِنْ حَيْثُ لَا يَعْلَمُونَ وَالرِّزْقُ مَقْسُومٌ وَهُوَ يَأْتِي ابْنَ آدَمَ عَلَى أَيِّ سِيرَةٍ سَارَهَا مِنَ الدُّنْيَا لَيْسَ تَقْوَى [متقي] مُتَّقٍ بِزَائِدِهِ وَلَا فُجُورُ فَاجِرٍ بِنَاقِصِهِ وَبَيْنَنَا وَبَيْنَهُ سِتْرٌ وَهُوَ طَالِبُهُ وَلَوْ أَنَّ أَحَدَكُمْ يَفِرُّ مِنْ رِزْقِهِ لَطَلَبَهُ رِزْقُهُ كَمَا يَطْلُبُهُ الْمَوْتُ.

He (Imām al-Riḍā, peace be upon him) continued: "Lord of the Worlds," is the Master of all creations, their Creator, and the One who brings their sustenance to them from sources they know and from sources they do not know. Provision is apportioned, and it reaches each child of Adam regardless of the way they live in this world. Neither the piety of a pious person will increase their sustenance, nor will the sinfulness of a sinner decrease it. There is a veil between us, and yet it seeks us. Even if a person was to flee from one's sustenance, it would pursue them just as death pursues them.

فَقَالَ اللَّهُ جَلَّ جَلَالُهُ: قُولُوا أَلْحَمْدُ لِلَّهِ عَلَى مَا أَنْعَمَ بِهِ عَلَيْنَا وَذَكَّرَنَا بِهِ مِنْ خَبَرٍ فِي كُتُبِ الْأَوَّلِينَ قَبْلَ أَنْ نَكُونَ فَفِي هٰذَا إِيجَابٌ عَلَى مُحَمَّدٍ وَآلِ مُحَمَّدٍ وَعَلَى شِيعَتِهِمْ أَنْ يَشْكُرُوهُ بِـمَا فَضَّلَهُمْ.

So, Allah, exalted be His Majesty, said: 'Say [all of you]: 'All praise belongs to Allah for what He has blessed us with, and reminded us about - from the accounts in the books of the ancients, before we even existed.' In this, there is an obligation upon Muḥammad and the family of Muḥammad, and their followers *(Shīʿas)* to thank Him for the favours He bestowed upon them.

وَذٰلِكَ أَنَّ رَسُولَ اللَّهِ صَلَّى اللَّهُ عَلَيْهِ وَآلِهِ وَسَلَّمَ: قَالَ لَمَّا بَعَثَ اللَّهُ عَزَّ وَجَلَّ مُوسَى بْنَ عِمْرَانَ عَلَيْهِ السَّلَامُ: وَاصْطَفَاهُ نَجِيًّا وَفَلَقَ لَهُ الْبَحْرَ وَنَجَّى بَنِي إِسْرَائِيلَ وَأَعْطَاهُ التَّوْرَاةَ وَالْأَلْوَاحَ وَرَأَى مَكَانَهُ مِنْ رَبِّهِ عَزَّ وَجَلَّ. فَقَالَ: يَا رَبِّ لَقَدْ أَكْرَمْتَنِي بِكَرَامَةٍ لَمْ تُكْرِمْ بِهَا أَحَدًا قَبْلِي.

This is because the Messenger of Allah, blessings of Allah be upon him and his family, said: 'When Allah, Exalted and Mighty, chose Mūsā ibn ʿImrān, peace be upon him, as His intimate friend, parted the sea for him, saved the Children of Isrāʾīl, gave him the Tawrāh and the tablets, and showed him his place with his Lord, he (Mūsā) said: 'O Lord, You honoured me with an honour that You have not given to anyone before me.''

فَقَالَ اللَّهُ جَلَّ جَلَالُهُ: يَا مُوسَى أَ مَا عَلِمْتَ أَنَّ مُحَمَّدًا أَفْضَلُ عِنْدِي مِنْ جَمِيعِ مَلَائِكَتِي وَجَمِيعِ خَلْقِي؟

So, Allah, Glorified and Exalted, replied: 'O Mūsā, do you not know that Muḥammad is more honoured with Me than all of My angels and all of My creations?'

قَالَ مُوسَى: يَا رَبِّ فَإِنْ كَانَ مُحَمَّدٌ أَكْرَمَ عِنْدَكَ مِنْ جَمِيعِ خَلْقِكَ فَهَلْ فِي آلِ الْأَنْبِيَاءِ أَكْرَمُ مِنْ آلِي؟

Mūsā asked: 'O Lord, if Muḥammad is more honoured in Your sight than all of Your creations, then is there anyone among the families of the Prophets more honoured than my family?'

قَالَ اللّٰهُ جَلَّ جَلَالُهُ: يَا مُوسَى أَ مَا عَلِمْتَ أَنَّ فَضْلَ آلِ مُحَمَّدٍ عَلَى جَمِيعِ النَّبِيِّينَ كَفَضْلِ مُحَمَّدٍ عَلَى جَمِيعِ الْمُرْسَلِينَ؟

Allah, exalted be His Majesty, replied: 'O Mūsā, do you not know that the superiority of the family of Muḥammad over all other families of the Prophets is like the superiority of Muḥammad over all of the Messengers?'

فَقَالَ مُوسَى: يَا رَبِّ فَإِنْ كَانَ آلُ مُحَمَّدٍ كَذٰلِكَ فَهَلْ فِي أُمَمِ الْأَنْبِيَاءِ أَفْضَلُ عِنْدَكَ مِنْ أُمَّتِي ظَلَّلْتَ عَلَيْهِمُ الْغَمَامَ وَأَنْزَلْتَ عَلَيْهِمُ الْمَنَّ وَالسَّلْوَى وَفَلَقْتَ لَهُمُ الْبَحْرَ.

Then Mūsā said: 'O Lord, if the family of Muḥammad holds such a rank, is there any nation among the nations of the Prophets more honoured in Your sight than my nation? You sheltered them with the clouds, sent down manna and quails for them, and parted the sea for them.'

فَقَالَ اللّٰهُ جَلَّ جَلَالُهُ: يَا مُوسَى أَ مَا عَلِمْتَ أَنَّ فَضْلَ أُمَّةِ مُحَمَّدٍ عَلَى جَمِيعِ الْأُمَمِ كَفَضْلِهِ عَلَى جَمِيعِ خَلْقِي؟

So, Allah, Glorified and Exalted, replied: 'O Mūsā, do you not know that the superiority of the nation of Muḥammad over all other nations is like his superiority over all of My creations?'

فَقَالَ مُوسَى: يَا رَبِّ لَيْتَنِي كُنْتُ أَرَاهُمْ.

Then Mūsā said: 'O Lord, I wish I could see them.'

فَأَوْحَى اللهُ عَزَّ وَجَلَّ إِلَيْهِ: يَا مُوسَى إِنَّكَ لَنْ تَرَاهُمْ وَلَيْسَ هٰذَا أَوَانَ ظُهُورِهِمْ وَلٰكِنْ سَوْفَ تَرَاهُمْ فِي الْجِنَانِ جَنَّاتِ عَدْنٍ وَالْفِرْدَوْسِ بِحَضْرَةِ مُحَمَّدٍ فِي نَعِيمِهَا يَتَقَلَّبُونَ وَفِي خَيْرَاتِهَا يَتَبَحْبَحُونَ أَ فَتُحِبُّ أَنْ أُسْمِعَكَ كَلَامَهُمْ؟

So, Allah, Mighty and Majestic, revealed to him: 'O Mūsā, you will not see them, for this is not the time for their emergence. But you will see them in the Gardens of Eden and in Paradise *(al-Firdaws)*, in the presence of Muḥammad, enjoying the blessings and indulging in its delights. Would you like Me to let you hear their words?'

قَالَ: نَعَمْ يَا إِلَهِي

Mūsā said: 'Yes, O my God.'

قَالَ اللهُ جَلَّ جَلَالُهُ: قُمْ بَيْنَ يَدَيَّ وَاشْدُدْ مِيزَرَكَ قِيَامَ الْعَبْدِ الذَّلِيلِ بَيْنَ يَدَيِ الْمَلِكِ الْجَلِيلِ.

Allah, Exalted and Majestic, said: 'Stand before Me and tighten your belt as a humble servant stands before a majestic king.'

فَفَعَلَ ذٰلِكَ مُوسَى عَلَيْهِ السَّلَامُ فَنَادَى: رَبُّنَا عَزَّ وَجَلَّ يَا أُمَّةَ مُحَمَّدٍ فَأَجَابُوهُ كُلُّهُمْ وَهُمْ فِي أَصْلَابِ آبَائِهِمْ وَأَرْحَامِ أُمَّهَاتِهِمْ لَبَّيْكَ اللَّهُمَّ لَبَّيْكَ لَا شَرِيكَ لَكَ لَبَّيْكَ إِنَّ الْحَمْدَ وَ النِّعْمَةَ لَكَ وَالْمُلْكَ لَا شَرِيكَ لَكَ.

Then Mūsā, peace be upon him, did so, and our Lord, Mighty and Majestic, called out: 'O nation of Muḥammad!' So, they all responded, even though they were still in the loins of their fathers and the wombs of their mothers, saying: *'Here we are, O Allah, here we are! You have no partner; here we are! Truly, all praise and blessings and sovereignty belong only to You; You have no partner.'*

قَالَ: فَجَعَلَ اللّٰهُ عَزَّ وَجَلَّ: تِلْكَ الْإِجَابَةَ شِعَارَ الْحَجِّ. ثُمَّ نَادَى رَبُّنَا تَعَالَى: يَا أُمَّةَ مُحَمَّدٍ إِنَّ قَضَائِي عَلَيْكُمْ أَنَّ رَحْمَتِي سَبَقَتْ غَضَبِي وَعَفْوِي قَبْلَ عِقَابِي فَقَدِ اسْتَجَبْتُ لَكُمْ مِنْ قَبْلِ أَنْ تَدْعُوَنِي وَأَعْطَيْتُكُمْ مِنْ قَبْلِ أَنْ تَسْأَلُونِي مَنْ لَقِيَنِي مِنْكُمْ بِشَهَادَةِ أَنْ لَا إِلٰهَ إِلَّا اللّٰهُ وَحْدَهُ لَا شَرِيكَ لَهُ وَأَنَّ مُحَمَّدًا عَبْدُهُ وَرَسُولُهُ صَادِقٌ فِي أَقْوَالِهِ مُحِقٌّ فِي أَفْعَالِهِ وَأَنَّ عَلِيَّ بْنَ أَبِي طَالِبٍ أَخُوهُ وَوَصِيُّهُ مِنْ بَعْدِهِ وَوَلِيُّهُ مُلْتَزَمٌ طَاعَتُهُ كَمَا يُلْزَمُ طَاعَةُ مُحَمَّدٍ وَأَنَّ أَوْلِيَاءَهُ الْمُصْطَفَيْنَ الْمُطَهَّرِينَ الْمَيَامِينَ بِعَجَائِبِ آيَاتِ اللّٰهِ وَدَلَائِلِ حُجَجِ اللّٰهِ مِنْ بَعْدِهِمَا أَوْلِيَاؤُهُ أُدْخِلُهُ جَنَّتِي وَإِنْ كَانَتْ ذُنُوبُهُ مِثْلَ زَبَدِ الْبَحْرِ.

He (Imām al-Riḍā, peace be upon him) said: 'Then Allah, Mighty and Majestic, made that response the slogan of *Ḥajj*. Our Lord, the All-High, then called out: 'O nation of Muḥammad, My decree upon you is that My mercy precedes My wrath, and My forgiveness comes before My punishment. I have responded to you before you called upon Me, and I have granted you before you asked. Whoever among you meets Me testifying that there is no god except Allah, alone without any partner, and that Muḥammad is His servant and His Messenger, truthful in his words, and just in his actions; and that 'Alī, son of Abū Ṭālib, is his brother, successor after him, and leader whose obedience is as obligatory as obedience to Muḥammad; and that his pure, chosen family, distinguished with the miraculous signs of Allah and proofs of Allah after them, are also His leaders – and I will admit them into My Paradise, even if their sins are as vast as the foam of the sea.'

قَالَ: فَلَمَّا بَعَثَ اللّٰهُ تَعَالَى مُحَمَّدٌ [مُحَمَّدًا] صَلَّى اللّٰهُ عَلَيْهِ وَآلِهِ وَسَلَّمَ قَالَ: يَا مُحَمَّدُ وَمَا كُنْتَ بِجَانِبِ الطُّورِ إِذْ نَادَيْنَا أُمَّتَكَ بِهٰذِهِ الْكَرَامَةِ. ثُمَّ قَالَ عَزَّ وَجَلَّ لِمُحَمَّدٍ: قُلْ

its administration are from Him, and He is the Nurturer and Sustainer of everything.

The meaning of *al-ʿĀlamīn* (the Worlds) either refers specifically to **human beings**, as in the Quran where we read that the angels said to Prophet Lūṭ ﷺ: "Did we not forbid you from [protecting] **people**?"[45]

It is also possible that it may refer to **all realms of existence.** The word *ʿālam* means creation, and *ʿĀlamīn* has been used to mean all creations.

From this verse, it is understood that all of existence has one Lord, and what was believed in the time of ignorance and among some nations that each type of phenomenon has its own god who manages and nurtures it is false.

أَلْحَمْدُ لِلّٰهِ رَبِّ الْعَالَمِينَ عَلَى مَا اخْتَصَّنِي بِهِ مِنْ هٰذِهِ الْفَضِيلَةِ وَقَالَ لِأُمَّتِهِ وَقُولُوا أَنْتُمْ الْحَمْدُ لِلّٰهِ رَبِّ الْعَالَمِينَ عَلَى مَا اخْتَصَّنَا بِهِ مِنْ هٰذِهِ الْفَضَائِلِ.

He (Imām al-Riḍā, peace be upon him) said: 'When Allah, Almighty, sent Muḥammad, blessings of Allah be upon him and his family, He said: 'O Muḥammad, and you were not on the side of Mount Sinai when We called your nation with this honour.' Then Allah, Mighty and Majestic, said to Muḥammad: 'Say: 'All praise belongs to Allah, Lord of the Worlds,' for this special honour which He granted me.'' And He said to his nation: 'And [all of you] too, say: 'All praise belongs to Allah, Lord of the Worlds,' for the virtues He has bestowed upon us.''"

[45] Quran, Sūrah al-Ḥijr (15), Verse 70:

﴿قَالُوٓاْ أَوَ لَمۡ نَنۡهَكَ عَنِ ٱلۡعَٰلَمِينَ ۝٧٠﴾

"They (the angels) said: 'Have we not forbidden you from (offering protection and interceding for) **people**?'"

Take Away Messages

1. All praise belongs to Allah ﷻ. In the word *'Alḥamdulillāh,'* the *'al-'* refers to all forms and types of praise.
2. Allah ﷻ does not force His creations as it relates to their nurturing and development [He provides the guidance they require, and they either accept it or reject it]. This must be understood as praise is only given for non-compulsory actions [meaning that if Allah ﷻ were to 'force' or 'compel' people to believe and follow His teachings, then it would be redundant to praise Him for something which His creations had no say in either accepting or rejecting. – Tr.]
3. All existence is beautiful, and the management of all existence is good, and praise is for beauty and goodness.
4. The reason for our praise is His Lordship.
5. The relationship of Allah ﷻ with creation is constant and intimate. When we refer to Allah ﷻ as Lord of the Worlds, we can contrast that to the example of a painter or builder. Once they complete their work and present it to society, they then leave. However, a true Nurturer maintains constant supervision – and only Allah ﷻ does that.
6. All existence is under the nurturing of One Being – not multiple gods – and that is only Allah ﷻ.
7. The potential for growth and development exists in all beings.

8. Allah ﷻ nurtures both human beings through Prophetic guidance – meaning through Legislative Nurturing *[al-Hidāyah al-Takwīnīyyah]*; and He develops minerals, plants, and animals through His Developmental Nurturing *[al-Hidāyah al-Tashrī'iyyah]*.
9. Believers begin the Book of Allah ﷻ – the Quran – with praise to Allah, the Exalted, saying: "'All praise belongs to Allah;' and at the end, when they enter Paradise, they will give the same proclamation: 'Their final call will be 'All praise belongs to Allah, Lord of the Worlds.''"[46]

[46] Quran, Sūrah Yūnus (10), Verse 10:
﴿دَعْوَىٰهُمْ فِيهَا سُبْحَـٰنَكَ ٱللَّهُمَّ وَتَحِيَّتُهُمْ فِيهَا سَلَـٰمٌ ۚ وَءَاخِرُ دَعْوَىٰهُمْ أَنِ ٱلْحَمْدُ لِلَّهِ رَبِّ ٱلْعَـٰلَمِينَ ۝١٠﴾
"Therein their invocation will be: 'All-Glorified You are, O Allah! (You are absolutely exalted above having any defects and doing anything wrong).' And their greeting (to each other, from Allah, and the angels) will be: 'Peace!' And their invocation will close with 'All praise (and gratitude) belongs to Allah, Lord of the Worlds!'"

Part III: A Compassionate Creator – Verse 3

أَلرَّحْمٰنِ الرَّحِيمِ

"The All-Compassionate, the All-Merciful."

Thinking Points

Allah ﷻ made Mercy binding upon Himself: "...Your Lord has prescribed upon Himself Mercy...;"[47] and His Mercy encompasses everything: "...And My Mercy extends to all things..."[48] Similarly, His final Messenger, Prophet Muḥammad ﷺ is also a source of mercy: "a mercy for all worlds;"[49] as is the Quran. His creation and nurturing are all based on Mercy, and even when He punishes, it is out of His intense Kindness.

---

[47] Quran, Sūrah al-Anʿām (6), Verse 54:

﴿...كَتَبَ رَبُّكُمْ عَلَىٰ نَفْسِهِ ٱلرَّحْمَةَ...﴾

[48] Quran, Sūrah al-Aʿrāf (7), Verse 156:

﴿...وَرَحْمَتِي وَسِعَتْ كُلَّ شَيْءٍ...﴾

[49] Quran, Sūrah al-Anbiyāʾ (21), Verse 107:

﴿وَمَآ أَرْسَلْنَٰكَ إِلَّا رَحْمَةً لِّلْعَٰلَمِينَ ١٠٧﴾

"And We have not sent you (O Muḥammad) but as an (unequalled) mercy to (all of) the worlds."

The forgiveness of sins, acceptance of His servants' repentance, concealment of their faults, and giving opportunities to make up for mistakes are all manifestations of His Mercy and Kindness.

This passage emphasizes the all-encompassing nature of the Mercy of Allah ﷻ, highlighting how it manifests in various ways – from creation to forgiveness, and even in punishment. It presents mercy as a fundamental Attribute of Allah ﷻ that influences all aspects of His interaction with creation.

Take Away Messages

1. Divine Management and Nurturing are accompanied by love and mercy – this is understood by the word *al-Raḥmān* – the All-Compassionate, appearing alongside the word *Rabb* – Nourisher and Sustainer.
2. Just as teaching requires compassion and kindness – "The All-Compassionate taught the Quran"[50] – nurturing and purification must also be based on compassion and kindness.
3. The Attribute of Allah ﷻ being All-Compassionate *(al-Raḥmān)* is ONE of the reasons why His creations should praise Him.

---

[50] Quran, Sūrah al-Raḥmān (55), Verses 1-2:

﴿ٱلرَّحْمَٰنُ ۝١ عَلَّمَ ٱلْقُرْءَانَ ۝٢﴾

"The All-Compassionate; He taught the Quran..."

Part IV: Day of Judgement – Verse 4

> مَالِكِ يَوْمِ الدِّينِ
>
> "Master of the Day of Judgement."

Thinking Points

The Ownership which Allah ﷻ possesses is real, and encompasses complete control and sovereignty, while conventional ownership, such as what people have, can escape the owner's control at any time, so it is not under their real authority.[51]

Although Allah ﷻ is always the true Owner of everything in this world, His Ownership will manifest differently on the Day of Judgement and in the Hereafter:

---

[51] An example of this is as follows: When a person buys a car, they "own" it. However, if they decide to sell it, or they pass away, then its ownership changes hands. The car was made by a certain car company and before they sold it, they owned it. The materials which make up the car, such as the fabric, plastic, electronics, glass, etc., were all owned by other companies and factories until they sold them to the car manufacturer. Thus, such ownership is not real authority, it is temporary. However, the ownership which Allah ﷻ has is real and permanent.

1. On that Day, all intermediaries and means will be cut off for the disbelievers: 'All of their ties will be cut off.'[52]
2. Relations and kinships cease to exist for the disbelievers: There will be no family ties between them.'[53]
3. Wealth and children will not benefit the disbelievers: 'Neither wealth, nor children will be of any benefit.'[54]
4. Relatives and close ones will not be able to provide any help: 'Your close relatives will not benefit you.'[55]

---

[52] Quran, Sūrah al-Baqarah (2), Verse 166:

﴿إِذْ تَبَرَّأَ ٱلَّذِينَ ٱتُّبِعُوا۟ مِنَ ٱلَّذِينَ ٱتَّبَعُوا۟ وَرَأَوُا۟ ٱلْعَذَابَ وَتَقَطَّعَتْ بِهِمُ ٱلْأَسْبَابُ ١٦٦﴾

"At that time those who were followed (in this world as elders, heads, or leaders, and loved as only Allah should be loved) will disown those who followed them, and declare themselves innocent of their evil deeds, and they will see the punishment, and the relations between them will be cut off."

[53] Quran, Sūrah al-Mu'minūn (23), Verse 101:

﴿فَإِذَا نُفِخَ فِى ٱلصُّورِ فَلَآ أَنسَابَ بَيْنَهُمْ يَوْمَئِذٍ وَلَا يَتَسَآءَلُونَ ١٠١﴾

"Then, when the Trumpet (of Resurrection) is blown, there will not be any ties of kinship among them (which will be of any avail) on that Day, nor will they ask about one another (as everyone will be too engrossed in their own plight to think about anyone else)."

[54] Quran, Sūrah al-Shuʿarā (26), Verse 88:

﴿يَوْمَ لَا يَنفَعُ مَالٌ وَلَا بَنُونَ ٨٨﴾

"The Day when neither wealth will be of any use, nor offspring."

[55] Quran, Sūrah al-Mumtaḥanah (60), Verse 3:

5. Neither will the disbelievers' tongues be allowed to make any excuses, nor will their minds have time to plan. The only solution will be the Grace of Allah ﷻ, as He is the authority of that Day.

The word *al-dīn* is used in various meanings in the Quran:

1. The collection of Divine Laws: 'Indeed, the (true) religion *(al-dīn)* with Allah is al-Islam.'[56]
2. Action and obedience: Sincere devotion is due to Allah.'[57]

﴿لَن تَنفَعَكُمْ أَرْحَامُكُمْ وَلَآ أَوْلَٰدُكُمْ ۚ يَوْمَ ٱلْقِيَٰمَةِ يَفْصِلُ بَيْنَكُمْ ۚ وَٱللَّهُ بِمَا
تَعْمَلُونَ بَصِيرٌ ٣﴾

"Never will your relatives, or your (own) children benefit you; on the Day of Resurrection, He will judge between you. And Allah Sees all that you do."

[56] Quran, Sūrah Āle 'Imrān (3), Verse 19:

﴿إِنَّ ٱلدِّينَ عِندَ ٱللَّهِ ٱلْإِسْلَٰمُ ۗ وَمَا ٱخْتَلَفَ ٱلَّذِينَ أُوتُوا۟ ٱلْكِتَٰبَ إِلَّا مِنۢ بَعْدِ مَا جَآءَهُمُ
ٱلْعِلْمُ بَغْيًۢا بَيْنَهُمْ ۗ وَمَن يَكْفُرْ بِـَٔايَٰتِ ٱللَّهِ فَإِنَّ ٱللَّهَ سَرِيعُ ٱلْحِسَابِ ١٩﴾

"Indeed, the (only true) religion with Allah is al-Islam. And those who were given the Book before differed only after the knowledge (of truth) came to them because of jealousy among themselves. And whoever disbelieves in the Signs of Allah (should know that) Allah is Swift at Reckoning."

[57] Quran, Sūrah al-Zumar (39), Verse 3:

﴿أَلَا لِلَّهِ ٱلدِّينُ ٱلْخَالِصُ ۚ وَٱلَّذِينَ ٱتَّخَذُوا۟ مِن دُونِهِۦٓ أَوْلِيَآءَ مَا نَعْبُدُهُمْ إِلَّا لِيُقَرِّبُونَآ إِلَى
ٱللَّهِ زُلْفَىٰٓ إِنَّ ٱللَّهَ يَحْكُمُ بَيْنَهُمْ فِى مَا هُمْ فِيهِ يَخْتَلِفُونَ ۗ إِنَّ ٱللَّهَ لَا يَهْدِى مَنْ هُوَ
كَٰذِبٌ كَفَّارٌ ٣﴾

3. Reckoning and recompense: "Master of the Day of Judgement."[58]

The phrase *'Yawm al-Dīn'* in the Quran means the Day of Judgement, which is the Day of Punishment and Reward, as the Quran notes that some people question: "They ask: 'When is the Day of Judgement?'"[59]

In introducing this Day, the Quran says: "Then, what can make you to perceive what the Day of Judgement is? It is the Day when no soul will have power to do anything for (in favour) of another; and the command on that Day will be for Allah (entirely and exclusively)."[60]

The usage of the phrase: "Master of the Day of Judgement" is a type of warning, but when placed alongside "The All-Compassionate, the All-Merciful," it shows that

---

"Unquestionably, for Allah alone is the pure religion [all sincere faith, worship, and obedience are due to Him only]. Yet, those who take, apart from Him, others (angels, *jinn*, or humans for guardians and confidants to entrust their affairs to) say: 'We worship them for no other reason than they may bring us nearer to Allah.' Indeed, Allah will judge between them concerning that which they differ. Indeed, Allah does not guide anyone who is a (determined) liar and an ingrate (confirmed disbeliever)."

58 Quran, Sūrah al-Fātiḥa (1), Verse 3:

﴿مَٰلِكِ يَوۡمِ ٱلدِّينِ ٤﴾

59 Quran, Sūrah al-Dhāriyāt (51), Verse 12:

﴿يَسۡـَٔلُونَ أَيَّانَ يَوۡمُ ٱلدِّينِ ١٢﴾

60 Quran, Sūrah al-Infiṭār (82), Verses 18-19:

﴿ثُمَّ مَآ أَدۡرَىٰكَ مَا يَوۡمُ ٱلدِّينِ ١٨ يَوۡمَ لَا تَمۡلِكُ نَفۡسٞ لِّنَفۡسٖ شَيۡـٔٗاۖ وَٱلۡأَمۡرُ يَوۡمَئِذٖ لِّلَّهِ ١٩
﴾

glad tidings and warnings should go together. Like another verse of the Quran which says: "Inform My servants that I am the All-Forgiving, the All-Merciful. And that it is My punishment which is indeed the painful punishment."[61] Likewise, in another verse, Allah ﷻ introduces Himself as: 'Acceptor of Repentance, Severe in Punishment.'[62]

In the first chapter of the Quran, Allah's Ownership *(Mālikiyyat)* is mentioned, where He says: "Master of the Day of Judgement;" and in the last chapter, His Kingship *(Malikiyyat)* is mentioned where He says: "King (or Sovereign) of humankind."[63]

Take Away Messages

1. Allah, the Exalted, is worthy of worship from different aspects, and we must offer His praise and gratitude:

---

61 Quran, Sūrah al-Ḥijr (15), Verses 49-50:

﴿نَبِّئْ عِبَادِىٓ أَنِّىٓ أَنَا ٱلْغَفُورُ ٱلرَّحِيمُ ۝٤٩ وَأَنَّ عَذَابِى هُوَ ٱلْعَذَابُ ٱلْأَلِيمُ ۝٥٠﴾

62 Quran, Sūrah Ghāfir (40), Verse 3:

﴿غَافِرِ ٱلذَّنۢبِ وَقَابِلِ ٱلتَّوْبِ شَدِيدِ ٱلْعِقَابِ ذِى ٱلطَّوْلِ ۖ لَآ إِلَٰهَ إِلَّا هُوَ ۖ إِلَيْهِ ٱلْمَصِيرُ ۝٣﴾

"The Forgiver of Sins and the Accepter of Repentance, (yet) Severe in Retribution, Limitless in His bounty. There is no deity except Him. To Him is the final return."

63 Quran, Sūrah al-Nās (114), Verse 2:

﴿مَلِكِ ٱلنَّاسِ ۝٢﴾

"The Sovereign of humankind."

- For the perfection of His Essence and Attributes, as He is "Allah."
- For His benevolence and nurturing, as He is Lord of the Worlds.
- For the hope and expectation of His Mercy and Kindness, as He is The All-Compassionate, The All-Merciful.
- For His Power and Majesty, as He is the Master of the Day of Judgement.

2. The Day of Judgement reflects His Lordship.
3. The Mercy of Allah ﷻ will manifest on the Day of Judgement.

Part V: Complete Worship – Verse 5

﴿إِيَّاكَ نَعْبُدُ وَإِيَّاكَ نَسْتَعِينُ﴾

"You (alone) do We worship, and You (alone) do we seek help."

Thinking Points

People should, by the mandate of reason, accept servitude to Allah ﷻ. We, human beings, love perfection and need growth and nurturing, and Allah ﷻ encompasses all perfections and is the Lord of all existence.

We need love and affection, and He is the All-Compassionate and the All-Merciful.

We should be worried about the distant future, but He is the Authority and Owner of that Day. So why should we turn to others when we have Him?!

Reason dictates that we should worship **only** Him and seek help **only** from Him, neither being slaves to our own desires, nor servants to others' wealth and power.

In *ṣalāt*, it is as if the person who is praying is representing all worshippers, when one says: "O Allah! Not just me, but all of us are Your servants; and not just me, but all of us need Your grace."

"O Allah! I have no one except You *(iyyāka)*, but You have many besides me, and all of existence are Your servants and slaves. You have said in the Quran: 'Everyone in the heavens and the Earth comes to the All-Merciful as a servant,'[64] and in reality, there is nothing in the heavens and Earth except that they are servants and obedient to Allah, the All-Merciful."

The phrase *"naʿbudu"* – we worship – indicates that ideally, *ṣalāt* should be offered in congregation, and that Muslims are all brethren of one another on the same path.

In this light, scholars of Islamic Spirituality note that the stages of spiritual flight are praise, connection, and then supplication. Therefore, the beginning of Sūrah al-Fātiḥa is praise, then the verse "You alone do we worship" *(iyyāka naʿbudu)* is connection, and the following verses are supplication.

Lastly, we must realize that conversation with the true Beloved, Allah ﷻ, is sweet; so perhaps for this reason, the word *"iyyāka"* (You alone) is repeated in this verse.

Take Away Messages

1. First, a person must worship Allah ﷻ, then ask for one's needs: we start by confirming that we worship only Him, then we ask Him for His help.
2. Worship is only appropriate before Allah ﷻ, not anyone else.
3. Although worship comes from us, we still need His help in everything – even worshipping.

---

[64] Quran, Sūrah Maryam (19), Verse 93:

﴿إِن كُلُّ مَن فِي ٱلسَّمَٰوَٰتِ وَٱلْأَرْضِ إِلَّآ ءَاتِي ٱلرَّحْمَٰنِ عَبْدًا ۝٩٣﴾

"There is none in the heavens and the Earth, except that they come to the All-Compassionate as a servant."

4. When we say that we only worship Him, and we only turn to Him for help, this means that there is neither compulsion, nor complete delegation in our lives. When we say: 'You alone do we worship,' it means that we have free will and are not compelled in life. When we say: 'We seek help from You alone,' it means that we need Him, and matters are not completely delegated to us – He plays a direct role in our lives.
5. Understanding Allah ﷻ and His Attributes is the prerequisite for achieving true Monotheism.
6. Among the etiquettes of supplication and worship is that a person should not put oneself forward as being "someone." Rather, a believer must feel themselves as constantly being a humble servant in the presence of Allah ﷻ.
7. When we develop an awareness of the Hereafter, then this will eventually lead to one of the motivations for worship of Allah ﷻ. "And we could not have been guided had Allah not guided us" – If it were not for Divine guidance, we would not be guided.[65]

---

[65] Quran, Sūrah al-Aʿrāf (7), Verse 43:

﴿وَنَزَعْنَا مَا فِي صُدُورِهِم مِّنْ غِلٍّ تَجْرِي مِن تَحْتِهِمُ ٱلْأَنْهَٰرُ ۖ وَقَالُوا۟ ٱلْحَمْدُ لِلَّهِ ٱلَّذِي
هَدَىٰنَا لِهَٰذَا وَمَا كُنَّا لِنَهْتَدِيَ لَوْلَآ أَنْ هَدَىٰنَا ٱللَّهُ ۖ لَقَدْ جَآءَتْ رُسُلُ رَبِّنَا بِٱلْحَقِّ ۖ وَنُودُوٓا۟
أَن تِلْكُمُ ٱلْجَنَّةُ أُورِثْتُمُوهَا بِمَا كُنتُمْ تَعْمَلُونَ ﴿٤٣﴾﴾

"And We will strip away whatever is in their hearts of resentment (rancor and any jealousy that they may have felt against other believers while in the world). Rivers flowing beneath them (and themselves overflowing with gratitude), and they will say: 'All praise (and gratitude) belong to Allah, Who has guided us to this (prosperity because of the guidance with which He favoured us in the world). If Allah had not guided us, we would certainly not have found the right way. Certainly, the Messengers of our Lord came with the Truth.' And a voice will call out to them: 'This is the Paradise that you have been made to inherit (in return) for what you used to do (in the world).'"

Part VI: The Straight Path – Verse 6

﴿إِهْدِنَا الصِّرَاطَ الْمُسْتَقِيمَ﴾

"Keep us on the Straight Path."

Thinking Points

In the Noble Quran, two types of guidance are discussed:

1. Developmental Guidance *(al-Hidāyah al-Takwīnīyyah)*, such as the guidance given to honeybees on how to extract nectar from flowers and build hives; or the guidance given to birds in their winter and summer migrations. This is what the Quran refers to when it says: "Our Lord is He Who gave everything its form and nature, then guided it aright."[66]
2. Legislative Guidance *(al-Hidāyah al-Tashri'īyyah)*, which is the deputation of Divinely-sent Prophets and Heavenly-sent Books for human guidance.

The word *"ṣirāṭ"* (path)[67] appears more than forty times in the Quran and choosing the right path and correct way

---

[66] Quran, Sūrah Ṭāhā (20), Verse 50:

﴿قَالَ رَبُّنَا ٱلَّذِىٓ أَعْطَىٰ كُلَّ شَىْءٍ خَلْقَهُۥ ثُمَّ هَدَىٰ ۝٥٠﴾

[67] The *ṣirāṭ*, when it refers to the next world is a bridge which passes over Hell which all people must pass over in order to get to Paradise.

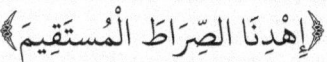

of thinking is a sign of the right development of human character.

Multiple non-Divine paths lie before human beings, from which they must choose one. Some of these paths include:

1. The path of personal desires and expectations.
2. The path of people's expectations and whims.
3. The path of Satan's temptations.
4. The path of tyrants.
5. The path of misguided ancestors and predecessors.
6. The path of Allah ﷻ and His close friends *(Awliyā')*.

A believing person chooses the path of Allah ﷻ and His close friends *(Awliyā')* over the above which has the following advantages:

1. The path of Allah ﷻ is constant and well defined – unlike the paths of tyrants, the desires of people, and personal whims – which change every day.
2. Allah ﷻ path is only one path, while the other paths are numerous and scattered.
3. A person is confident in both the path and its destination.
4. There is no failure or loss in following the path of Allah ﷻ.

The Quran makes it clear that the Straight Path is:

1. The Path of Allah ﷻ: "Indeed, my Lord is on a Straight Path."[68]

---

[68] Quran, Sūrah Hūd (11), Verse 56:

2. The Path of the Prophets: "Indeed, you (Muḥammad) are one of the Messengers. Upon a Straight Path."[69]
3. The Path of worshipping Allah ﷻ: "And worship Me (alone); this is a Straight Path."[70]
4. Reliance and trust in Allah ﷻ: "And whoever holds firmly to Allah has certainly been guided to a Straight Path."[71]
5. Monotheism and seeking help only from Him.[72]
6. The Book of Allah ﷻ.[73]
7. The path of a sound nature.[74]

A person must seek help from Allah ﷻ both in choosing the Straight Path and remaining steadfast on it, just like a lamp that constantly receives its light from a power source; and

---

﴿إِنَّ رَبِّي عَلَىٰ صِرَاطٍ مُّسْتَقِيمٍ ۝٥٦﴾

[69] Quran, Sūrah Yāsīn (36), Verses 3-4:

﴿إِنَّكَ لَمِنَ ٱلْمُرْسَلِينَ ۝٣ عَلَىٰ صِرَاطٍ مُّسْتَقِيمٍ ۝٤﴾

[70] Quran, Sūrah Yāsīn (36), Verse 61:

﴿وَأَنِ ٱعْبُدُونِي ۚ هَٰذَا صِرَاطٌ مُّسْتَقِيمٌ ۝٦١﴾

[71] Quran, Sūrah Āle ʿImrān (3), Verse 101:

﴿...وَمَن يَعْتَصِم بِٱللَّهِ فَقَدْ هُدِيَ إِلَىٰ صِرَاطٍ مُّسْتَقِيمٍ ۝١٠١﴾

[72] The *alif* and *lām* which appears at the front of the word *ṣirāṭ* refers to the fact that this is the only path of Monotheism as was seen in the previous verse. Quran, Sūrah al-Fātiḥa (1), Verse 6.

[73] According to a *ḥadīth* found in *Tafsīr Majmaʿ al-Bayān*, Vol. 1, Pg. 58.

[74] According to a *ḥadīth* from Imam Jaʿfar al-Ṣādiq ؑ found in *Tafsir al-Ṣāfī*, Vol. 1, Pg. 86.

for this reason, a minimum of ten times a day, we repeat: "Keep us on the Straight Path."[75]

Continuing to remain on the Straight Path is the only request that Muslims ask from Allah ﷻ in every prayer; and it is something which even Prophet Muḥammad ﷺ and the Immaculate Imams عليهم السلام prayed for – steadfastness on the Straight Path from Allah ﷻ.

A person should always pray to Allah ﷻ for the Straight Path in all aspects of one's life, whether it be choosing friends, a particular field of study, a job, or a spouse. This is because one might think correctly as far as their beliefs are concerned, but may slip in their actions, or vice versa. Therefore, continuously asking Allah ﷻ for the Straight Path is extremely important.

The Straight Path has different levels and stages. Even those who are on the Right Path, such as the close friends of Allah ﷻ *(Awliyā')*, need to continuously ask to remain on the path, and pray for an increase in the light of guidance. "And those who are guided, He increases them in guidance."[76]

---

[75] Quran, Sūrah al-Fātiḥa (1), Verse 6:

﴿ٱهۡدِنَا ٱلصِّرَٰطَ ٱلۡمُسۡتَقِيمَ ٦﴾

[76] Those who ask for this have passed some of the stages of guidance, and thus, their request is now for them to be guided to the next, higher stages. See Quran, Sūrah Muḥammad (47), Verse 17:

﴿وَٱلَّذِينَ ٱهۡتَدَوۡاْ زَادَهُمۡ هُدٗى وَءَاتَىٰهُمۡ تَقۡوَىٰهُمۡ ١٧﴾

In addition, the Straight Path is a balanced and middle way, as Imam ʿAlī ﷺ says: "The right and the left are misleading, but the middle way is the true road (the path of guidance)."[77]

The Straight Path means moderation and balance, avoiding any kind of excess or shortcomings, whether in belief or in action:

1. One person may deviate in their beliefs, while another in their actions and morals.
2. One attributes everything to Allah ﷻ as if humans have no role in their own fate, while another considers themselves to be in complete control and sees the Hand of Allah ﷻ as inactive.
3. One introduces Divinely sent leaders as ordinary people, sometimes even labeling them as sorcerers or insane, while another raises these great personalities to the level of God!
4. One considers the visitation to the graves of the Imams and martyrs as an innovation, while another ties ropes to trees and walls, seeking intercession from them.
5. One views the economy as the foundation of everything, while another ignores the affairs of this world entirely.

"And as for those who are guided, He increases them in guidance and gives them their righteous (piety and protection from sinning)."

[77] *Biḥār al-Anwār*, Vol. 87, Pg. 3.

6. In practice, one shows misplaced jealousy, while another sends his wife out into the streets without *ḥijāb* or modest clothing.
7. One is miserly, while another gives away wealth recklessly.
8. One distances oneself from people, while another sacrifices the truth for the sake of people.

Such behaviours and actions are deviations from the Straight Path of guidance, and thus, Allah ﷻ introduces His firm and established religion as the Straight Path.[78]

In narrations, the Immaculate Imams ﵇ have said: "The Straight Path is us"[79] – meaning that the living, practical example of the Straight Path, and the true models to follow, are the Heavenly leaders sent by Allah ﷻ for the guidance of humanity. They provided guidance on every aspect of life, such as work, leisure, study, food, charity, criticism, conflict, peace, love for children, and so much more, advising us to follow moderation and balance in all these areas.[80]

---

[78] Quran, Sūrah al-Anʿām (6), Verse 161:

﴿قُلۡ إِنَّنِي هَدَىٰنِي رَبِّيٓ إِلَىٰ صِرَٰطٖ مُّسۡتَقِيمٖ دِينٗا قِيَمٗا مِّلَّةَ إِبۡرَٰهِيمَ حَنِيفٗاۚ وَمَا كَانَ مِنَ ٱلۡمُشۡرِكِينَ ١٦١﴾

"Say: 'Indeed, my Lord has guided me to a Straight Path, being an upright Religion [leading to prosperity in both worlds], the way of Ibrāhīm based on pure faith. He was never among those who associated partners (with Allah).'"

[79] *Tafsīr Nūr al-Thaqalayn*, Vol. 1, Pg. 20.

[80] In this regard, we can refer to the book, *Uṣūl al-Kāfī* by Shaykh Kulaynī on the section of Moderation in Worship.

Lastly, interestingly, Satan lies on this very Straight Path to ambush and misguide humanity![81]

In the Quran and narrations, there are many examples that emphasize moderation, and warn against excess and deficiency in all areas of life. Consider the following:

1. "And eat and drink, but do not be wasteful. Indeed, He does not love those who waste."[82]
2. When giving charity, do not be stingy, but also do not be so generous that you become in need yourself. "And do not keep your hand tightly chained to your neck, nor stretch it out fully (otherwise) you will be blamed and regretful."[83]
3. "And those who, when they spend, are neither extravagant nor miserly, but take a moderate stance in between."[84] Believers, when they spend, are neither wasteful, nor stingy, but balanced.

---

[81] Satan is quoted in the Quran in Sūrah al-Aʿrāf (7), Verse 16 as having said the following to Allah ﷻ:

﴿قَالَ فَبِمَآ أَغْوَيْتَنِى لَأَقْعُدَنَّ لَهُمْ صِرَٰطَكَ ٱلْمُسْتَقِيمَ ﴿١٦﴾﴾

"He (Iblis) said: 'Since You allowed me to (rebel and) go astray, I will surely lie in wait for them (humankind) on Your Straight Path (to lure them away from it).'"

[82] Quran, Sūrah al-Aʿrāf (7), Verse 31:

﴿... وَكُلُوا۟ وَٱشْرَبُوا۟ وَلَا تُسْرِفُوٓا۟ ۚ إِنَّهُۥ لَا يُحِبُّ ٱلْمُسْرِفِينَ ﴿٣١﴾﴾

[83] Quran, Sūrah al-Isrāʾ (17), Verse 29:

﴿وَلَا تَجْعَلْ يَدَكَ مَغْلُولَةً إِلَىٰ عُنُقِكَ وَلَا تَبْسُطْهَا كُلَّ ٱلْبَسْطِ فَتَقْعُدَ مَلُومًا مَّحْسُورًا ﴿٢٩﴾﴾

[84] Quran, Sūrah al-Furqān (25), Verse 67:

﴿وَٱلَّذِينَ إِذَآ أَنفَقُوا۟ لَمْ يُسْرِفُوا۟ وَلَمْ يَقْتُرُوا۟ وَكَانَ بَيْنَ ذَٰلِكَ قَوَامًا ﴿٦٧﴾﴾

4. "...And do not raise your voice too loud in prayer, nor make it too quiet, but seek a middle course."[85] When a person recites *ṣalāt*, one should pray in a moderate tone – not too loud, nor too soft.
5. Be kind to your parents: "And be good to your parents;"[86] however, if they try to lead you away from the path of Allah, then obeying them is not required: "But if they strive to make you associate with Me, then do not obey them..."[87]
6. The final Prophet ﷺ was given a universal mission: 'And he was a Messenger and a Prophet;'[88] but he also invited his own family: "And command your family to pray, and be diligent in its observance."[89]
7. Islam encourages both *ṣalāt*, which connects a person to the Creator: "Establish prayer;" and *zakāt*,

---

[85] Quran, Sūrah al-Isrā' (17), Verse 110:

﴿...وَلَا تَجْهَرْ بِصَلَاتِكَ وَلَا تُخَافِتْ بِهَا وَابْتَغِ بَيْنَ ذَٰلِكَ سَبِيلًا ﴿١١٠﴾﴾

[86] Quran, Sūrah al-Isrā' (17), Verse 23:

﴿...وَبِالْوَالِدَيْنِ إِحْسَانًا...﴾

[87] Quran, Sūrah Luqmān (31), Verse 15:

﴿وَإِن جَاهَدَاكَ عَلَىٰ أَن تُشْرِكَ بِي مَا لَيْسَ لَكَ بِهِ عِلْمٌ فَلَا تُطِعْهُمَا... ﴿١٥﴾﴾

[88] Quran, Sūrah al-Aḥzāb (33), Verse 40:

﴿مَا كَانَ مُحَمَّدٌ أَبَا أَحَدٍ مِنْ رِجَالِكُمْ وَلَٰكِنْ رَسُولَ اللَّهِ وَخَاتَمَ النَّبِيِّينَ وَكَانَ اللَّهُ بِكُلِّ شَيْءٍ عَلِيمًا ﴿٤٠﴾﴾

[89] Quran, Sūrah Ṭāhā (20), Verse 132:

﴿وَأْمُرْ أَهْلَكَ بِالصَّلَاةِ وَاصْطَبِرْ عَلَيْهَا... ﴿١٣٢﴾﴾

which is about connecting with people: "Give charity."[90]

8. Do not let your love for someone lead you away from bearing true testimony: "Be witnesses for Allah, even if it is against your own selves;[91] and do not let hatred drive you away from justice: "And do not let the enmity of a people prevent you from being just. Be just, that is nearer to righteousness."[92]
9. Believers have both a sense of repulsion: "Harsh towards the disbelievers" and attraction: "Merciful among themselves."[93]
10. Both faith and inner belief are necessary: "They believe;" as well as perform righteous actions: "They do good, virtuous deeds;"[94] then glad tidings will be given to them.

---

[90] Quran, Sūrah al-Baqarah (2), Verse 43:

﴿وَأَقِيمُواْ ٱلصَّلَوٰةَ وَءَاتُواْ ٱلزَّكَوٰةَ...٤٣﴾

"Establish the prayer *(ṣalāt)* and pay the charity (*zakāt).*"

[91] Quran, Sūrah al-Nisā' (4), Verse 135:

﴿...كُونُواْ قَوَّٰمِينَ بِٱلْقِسْطِ شُهَدَآءَ لِلَّهِ وَلَوْ عَلَىٰٓ أَنفُسِكُمْ...﴾

"...Be upholders of justice, witnesses for (the sake of) Allah, even though it be against your own selves..."

[92] Quran, Sūrah al-Mā'idah (5), Verse 8:

﴿...وَلَا يَجْرِمَنَّكُمْ شَنَـَٔانُ قَوْمٍ عَلَىٰٓ أَلَّا تَعْدِلُواْ ٱعْدِلُواْ هُوَ أَقْرَبُ لِلتَّقْوَىٰ...﴾

[93] Quran, Sūrah al-Fatḥ (48), Verse 29:

﴿...وَٱلَّذِينَ مَعَهُۥٓ أَشِدَّآءُ عَلَى ٱلْكُفَّارِ رُحَمَآءُ بَيْنَهُمْ...﴾

[94] Quran, Sūrah al-Baqarah (2), Verse 25:

﴿وَبَشِّرِ ٱلَّذِينَ ءَامَنُواْ وَعَمِلُواْ ٱلصَّٰلِحَٰتِ...﴾

11. Tears, prayers, and seeking victory from Allah ﷻ are all important: "Our Lord, pour down patience upon us, and make our feet firm;"[95] and so is perseverance and endurance in hardships: "Twenty patient people can vanquish two hundred."[96] On the Night of ʿĀshūrāʾ, Imam Ḥusayn ﵇ engaged in both supplications, as well as sharpening his sword.
12. On the Day of ʿArafah and the Night of ʿEid al-Aḍḥā, pilgrims recite prayers; but then on ʿEid, they must also sacrifice in the way of Allah ﷻ.
13. Islam acknowledges ownership: "People have authority over their own wealth;"[97] but it does not allow usurping from or harming others, and it limits authority: "There should be neither harm, nor causing of any harm."[98]

In conclusion, we see that Islam is not a one-dimensional religion that focuses only on one aspect, while neglecting others. Rather, in every situation and instance, it advises moderation, balance, and following the Straight Path.

---

[95] Quran, Sūrah al-Baqarah (2), Verse 250:

﴿...رَبَّنَآ أَفۡرِغۡ عَلَيۡنَا صَبۡرٗا وَثَبِّتۡ أَقۡدَامَنَا...﴾

[96] Quran, Sūrah al-Anfāl (8), Verse 65:

﴿...إِن يَكُن مِّنكُمۡ عِشۡرُونَ صَٰبِرُونَ يَغۡلِبُواْ مِاْئَتَيۡنِۚ...﴾

"...If there are among you twenty (who are) steadfast, they will overcome two hundred..."

[97] *Biḥār al-Anwār*, Vol. 2, Pg. 272.

[98] *Uṣūl al-Kāfī*, Vol. 5, Pg. 28.

Take Away Messages

1. All of creation is moving along the path that Allah ﷻ has Willed. O Allah! Place us on the path that You love.
2. Seeking guidance to and remaining on the Straight Path is the most important request of monotheists.
3. To attain the Straight Path, one must pray for it.
4. First comes praise, then seeking help and supplication.
5. The best example of seeking help from Allah ﷻ is asking for the Straight Path.

Part VII: Deviation in Beliefs – Verse 7

﴿صِرَاطَ الَّذِينَ أَنْعَمْتَ عَلَيْهِمْ غَيْرِ الْمَغْضُوبِ عَلَيْهِمْ وَلَا الضَّالِّينَ﴾

"The Path of those whom You have favoured, not of those who have incurred (Your) wrath (punishment and condemnation), nor of those who are astray."

Points

This verse introduces *The Straight Path* as the route of those who have been blessed by Allah ﷻ, which includes the Prophets *(al-Nabīyyīn)*, the truthful ones *(al-Ṣiddīqīn)*, the martyrs *(al-Shuhadāʾ)*, and the righteous ones *(al-Ṣāliḥīn)*.[99]

Reflecting on the path of these great individuals and aspiring to follow it, while reinforcing this desire within

---

[99] Quran, Sūrah al-Nisā (4), Verse 69:

﴿وَمَن يُطِعِ ٱللَّهَ وَٱلرَّسُولَ فَأُو۟لَٰٓئِكَ مَعَ ٱلَّذِينَ أَنْعَمَ ٱللَّهُ عَلَيْهِم مِّنَ ٱلنَّبِيِّـۧنَ وَٱلصِّدِّيقِينَ وَٱلشُّهَدَآءِ وَٱلصَّٰلِحِينَ ۚ وَحَسُنَ أُو۟لَٰٓئِكَ رَفِيقًا ۝٦٩﴾

"And whoever obeys Allah and the Messenger (as they must be obeyed), then those are the ones upon whom Allah has favoured (with the perfect guidance) – the Prophets, and the truthful ones, and the witnesses, and the righteous ones. How excellent are those for companions!"

ourselves, keeps us from the danger of deviation, and falling in misleading directions that people may take in life.

After this request, there is a plea to Allah ﷻ not to place us on the path of those who have incurred His wrath, or those who have gone astray. This is because many were granted the blessings of Allah ﷻ, but due to their ingratitude and stubbornness, they became subject to His wrath. A prime example of this in the Quran are the Children of Isrāʾīl.[100]

In this verse, the Quran divides people into three groups:

1. Those who have received the blessing of guidance and remain steadfast.
2. Those who have incurred wrath.
3. Those who have gone astray.

The meaning of "blessing" in "whom You have blessed" refers to the blessing of guidance. This is because the previous verse spoke about guidance, but material blessings are also possessed by disbelievers, deviants, and others, so it cannot be material blessings that are being referred to here.

Even those who are guided by Allah ﷻ face risks in life, thus we must constantly ask Allah ﷻ to prevent us from deviating from the Straight Path or going towards the way of His wrath and misguidance.

---

[100] Quran, Sūrah Maryam (19), Verse 59:

﴿فَخَلَفَ مِنۢ بَعۡدِهِمۡ خَلۡفٌ أَضَاعُواْ ٱلصَّلَوٰةَ وَٱتَّبَعُواْ ٱلشَّهَوَٰتِۖ فَسَوۡفَ يَلۡقَوۡنَ غَيًّا ٥٩﴾

"Then, there succeeded them generations who neglected the prayer and followed (their) desires, so they will meet perdition."

The Recipients of Wrath

In the Quran, individuals such as Pharaoh, Qārūn, and Abū Lahab; and nations like the people of ʿĀd, Thamūd, and the Children of Isrāʾīl, are introduced as those who have incurred the Wrath of Allah ﷻ. In several verses of this Divine Book, the characteristics of the misguided and those upon whom anger has been brought, as well as their examples, have been mentioned. Some examples include the following:

Hypocrites, polytheists, and those who harboured doubts about Allah ﷻ: "Indeed, Allah does not forgive that partners be associated with Him; but He forgives what is less than that for whomever He Wills. And whoever associates partners with Allah has indeed strayed far away (from the Straight Path)."[101]

Also, the Quran states: "And that He may punish the hypocritical men and the hypocritical women, and the polytheist men and the polytheist women – those who entertain evil thoughts about Allah. Theirs will be the evil turn of fate. Allah has become angry with them and has (eternally) excluded them from His Mercy, and prepared Hell for them. How evil a destination it is (to arrive at)!"[102]

---

[101] Quran, Sūrah al-Nisā' (4), Verse 116:

﴿إِنَّ ٱللَّهَ لَا يَغۡفِرُ أَن يُشۡرَكَ بِهِۦ وَيَغۡفِرُ مَا دُونَ ذَٰلِكَ لِمَن يَشَآءُۚ وَمَن يُشۡرِكۡ بِٱللَّهِ فَقَدۡ ضَلَّ ضَلَٰلَۢا بَعِيدًا ١١٦﴾

[102] Quran, Sūrah al-Fatḥ (48), Verse 6:

Disbelievers in Allah's ﷻ signs and killers of His Prophets: "And (remember the time) when you said: 'O Mūsā, we can no longer endure one sort of food. So, call upon your Lord, that He may bring forth for us from the earth its green herbs, and its cucumbers, and its garlic, and its lentils, and its onions.' He (Mūsā) responded: 'Would you exchange what is better for what is less? Go into (any) settlement, surely there is for you there what you ask for.' So, in the end, they were covered with humiliation and poverty, and they earned wrath (a humiliating punishment) from Allah. That was because they persistently disbelieved in Our Revelations and rejected Our signs, and they killed the Prophets without right. That was because they disobeyed and kept on exceeding the bounds (of the Law)."[103]

People of the Book (Jews and Christians) who rebel against the call to truth: "(O Community of Muḥammad ﷺ!) You are the best community ever brought forth for (as

---

﴿وَيُعَذِّبَ ٱلْمُنَـٰفِقِينَ وَٱلْمُنَـٰفِقَـٰتِ وَٱلْمُشْرِكِينَ وَٱلْمُشْرِكَـٰتِ ٱلظَّآنِّينَ بِٱللَّهِ ظَنَّ ٱلسَّوْءِ ۚ عَلَيْهِمْ دَآئِرَةُ ٱلسَّوْءِ ۖ وَغَضِبَ ٱللَّهُ عَلَيْهِمْ وَلَعَنَهُمْ وَأَعَدَّ لَهُمْ جَهَنَّمَ ۖ وَسَآءَتْ مَصِيرًا ۝٦﴾

[103] Quran, Sūrah al-Baqarah (2), Verse 61:
﴿وَإِذْ قُلْتُمْ يَـٰمُوسَىٰ لَن نَّصْبِرَ عَلَىٰ طَعَامٍ وَٰحِدٍ فَٱدْعُ لَنَا رَبَّكَ يُخْرِجْ لَنَا مِمَّا تُنۢبِتُ ٱلْأَرْضُ مِنۢ بَقْلِهَا وَقِثَّآئِهَا وَفُومِهَا وَعَدَسِهَا وَبَصَلِهَا ۖ قَالَ أَتَسْتَبْدِلُونَ ٱلَّذِى هُوَ أَدْنَىٰ بِٱلَّذِى هُوَ خَيْرٌ ۚ ٱهْبِطُوا۟ مِصْرًا فَإِنَّ لَكُم مَّا سَأَلْتُمْ ۗ وَضُرِبَتْ عَلَيْهِمُ ٱلذِّلَّةُ وَٱلْمَسْكَنَةُ وَبَآءُو بِغَضَبٍ مِّنَ ٱللَّهِ ۗ ذَٰلِكَ بِأَنَّهُمْ كَانُوا۟ يَكْفُرُونَ بِـَٔايَـٰتِ ٱللَّهِ وَيَقْتُلُونَ ٱلنَّبِيِّـۧنَ بِغَيْرِ ٱلْحَقِّ ۗ ذَٰلِكَ بِمَا عَصَوا۟ وَّكَانُوا۟ يَعْتَدُونَ ۝٦١﴾

an example for) humankind, enjoining what is right, and forbidding evil, and you believe in Allah. If only the People of the Book believed (as you do), this would have been better for them. Among them, there are (some) believers, but most of them are transgressors. They will never be able to harm you except hurting a little (mostly with their tongues). And if they fight against you, they will turn their backs in flight; then they will not be helped. Ignominy has been their portion wherever they have been found except for (when they hold on to) a rope from Allah, or a rope from other people; and they were visited with a wrath (humiliating punishment) from Allah, and misery is upon them – and all this because they persistently disbelieved in Our Revelations, and rejected Our signs of truth, and killed the Prophets against all right; and all of this because they disobeyed and kept on transgressing (the bounds of the Law)."[104]

Those who flee from *jihād*: "And whoever turns their back on them on such a day – except that it be tactical maneuvering to fight again or joining (another) troop of believers (or taking up a position against another enemy

---

[104] Quran, Surah Āle ʿImrān (3), Verses 110–112:

﴿كُنتُمْ خَيْرَ أُمَّةٍ أُخْرِجَتْ لِلنَّاسِ تَأْمُرُونَ بِٱلْمَعْرُوفِ وَتَنْهَوْنَ عَنِ ٱلْمُنكَرِ وَتُؤْمِنُونَ
بِٱللَّهِ ۗ وَلَوْ ءَامَنَ أَهْلُ ٱلْكِتَـٰبِ لَكَانَ خَيْرًا لَّهُم ۚ مِّنْهُمُ ٱلْمُؤْمِنُونَ وَأَكْثَرُهُمُ ٱلْفَـٰسِقُونَ ﴿١١٠﴾
لَن يَضُرُّوكُمْ إِلَّآ أَذًى ۖ وَإِن يُقَـٰتِلُوكُمْ يُوَلُّوكُمُ ٱلْأَدْبَارَ ثُمَّ لَا يُنصَرُونَ ﴿١١١﴾ ضُرِبَتْ عَلَيْهِمُ
ٱلذِّلَّةُ أَيْنَ مَا ثُقِفُوٓا۟ إِلَّا بِحَبْلٍ مِّنَ ٱللَّهِ وَحَبْلٍ مِّنَ ٱلنَّاسِ وَبَآءُو بِغَضَبٍ مِّنَ ٱللَّهِ
وَضُرِبَتْ عَلَيْهِمُ ٱلْمَسْكَنَةُ ۚ ذَٰلِكَ بِأَنَّهُمْ كَانُوا۟ يَكْفُرُونَ بِـَٔايَـٰتِ ٱللَّهِ وَيَقْتُلُونَ ٱلْأَنۢبِيَآءَ
بِغَيْرِ حَقٍّ ۚ ذَٰلِكَ بِمَا عَصَوا۟ وَّكَانُوا۟ يَعْتَدُونَ ﴿١١٢﴾﴾

host) – has indeed incurred the wrath of Allah, and their final refuge will be the Fire; how wretched a destination (to arrive at)."[105]

Those who accept, but then replace faith with disbelief: "Or do you desire to harass your Messenger (with senseless questions and unanswerable demands such as seeing Allah plainly) as Mūsā was harassed before? Whoever exchanges faith for disbelief has certainly strayed from the right way."[106]

Also, the Quran states: "Whoever disbelieves in (denies) Allah after having believed – except the one who is under duress (forced to renounce their religion), while their heart is firm and content with faith; but the one who willingly opens up their heart to disbelief – upon them is the wrath of Allah, and for them is a mighty punishment."[107]

Those who take the enemies of Allah ﷻ as allies and seek relationships with them: "O you who believe! Do not take My enemies and your enemies as friends, extending to them love and affection, while they have

---

[105] Quran, Sūrah al-Anfāl (8), Verse 16:

﴿وَمَن يُوَلِّهِمْ يَوْمَئِذٍ دُبُرَهُۥٓ إِلَّا مُتَحَرِّفًا لِّقِتَالٍ أَوْ مُتَحَيِّزًا إِلَىٰ فِئَةٍ فَقَدْ بَآءَ بِغَضَبٍ مِّنَ ٱللَّهِ وَمَأْوَىٰهُ جَهَنَّمُ ۖ وَبِئْسَ ٱلْمَصِيرُ ۝١٦﴾

[106] Quran, Sūrah al-Baqarah (2), Verse 108:

﴿أَمْ تُرِيدُونَ أَن تَسْـَٔلُوا۟ رَسُولَكُمْ كَمَا سُئِلَ مُوسَىٰ مِن قَبْلُ ۗ وَمَن يَتَبَدَّلِ ٱلْكُفْرَ بِٱلْإِيمَـٰنِ فَقَدْ ضَلَّ سَوَآءَ ٱلسَّبِيلِ ۝١٠٨﴾

[107] Quran, Sūrah al-Naḥl (16), Verse 106:

﴿مَن كَفَرَ بِٱللَّهِ مِنۢ بَعْدِ إِيمَـٰنِهِۦٓ إِلَّا مَنْ أُكْرِهَ وَقَلْبُهُۥ مُطْمَئِنٌّۢ بِٱلْإِيمَـٰنِ وَلَـٰكِن مَّن شَرَحَ بِٱلْكُفْرِ صَدْرًا فَعَلَيْهِمْ غَضَبٌ مِّنَ ٱللَّهِ وَلَهُمْ عَذَابٌ عَظِيمٌ ۝١٠٦﴾

disbelieved in the truth that has come to you, having driven out the Messenger and yourselves away (from your homes) only because you believe in Allah, your Lord (Who created you and sustains you). If you (now) have set forth (from your homes) to strive in My way, and to seek My approval (and good pleasure), (so do not take them for friends). You confide in them affection (out of your love and friendship), but I am better aware (than yourselves) of what you do in secret, as well as of what you disclose. And whoever does it among you has surely strayed from the right way."[108]

The Children of Isrā'īl, whose story and civilization are narrated multiple times in the Quran, were once superior to the people of their time: "I favoured you over all others…"[109]

---

108 Quran, Sūrah al-Mumtaḥanah (60) Verse 1:

﴿يَٰٓأَيُّهَا ٱلَّذِينَ ءَامَنُواْ لَا تَتَّخِذُواْ عَدُوِّي وَعَدُوَّكُمۡ أَوۡلِيَآءَ تُلۡقُونَ إِلَيۡهِم بِٱلۡمَوَدَّةِ وَقَدۡ كَفَرُواْ بِمَا جَآءَكُم مِّنَ ٱلۡحَقِّ يُخۡرِجُونَ ٱلرَّسُولَ وَإِيَّاكُمۡ أَن تُؤۡمِنُواْ بِٱللَّهِ رَبِّكُمۡ إِن كُنتُمۡ خَرَجۡتُمۡ جِهَٰدٗا فِي سَبِيلِي وَٱبۡتِغَآءَ مَرۡضَاتِيۚ تُسِرُّونَ إِلَيۡهِم بِٱلۡمَوَدَّةِ وَأَنَا۠ أَعۡلَمُ بِمَآ أَخۡفَيۡتُمۡ وَمَآ أَعۡلَنتُمۡۚ وَمَن يَفۡعَلۡهُ مِنكُمۡ فَقَدۡ ضَلَّ سَوَآءَ ٱلسَّبِيلِ ١﴾

109 Quran, Sūrah al-Baqarah (2), Verse 47:

﴿يَٰبَنِيٓ إِسۡرَٰٓءِيلَ ٱذۡكُرُواْ نِعۡمَتِيَ ٱلَّتِيٓ أَنۡعَمۡتُ عَلَيۡكُمۡ وَأَنِّي فَضَّلۡتُكُمۡ عَلَى ٱلۡعَٰلَمِينَ ٤٧﴾

"O Children of Isrā'īl! Remember My favour that I bestowed upon you, and that I once exalted you over the worlds (above all people)."

However, after this distinction and superiority, due to their own actions, they incurred the anger and wrath of Allah ﷻ: "They incurred the wrath of Allah."[110]

This change in their fate was a result of their behaviour and actions. Jewish scholars altered the Divine Laws and Commandments of the Tawrah: "They distort the words."[111] Their merchants and wealthy individuals turned to usury, unlawful earnings, and a life of luxury: "They took interest."[112]

Meanwhile, the public, out of laziness and fear, refused to go to the battlefield and enter the sacred land when called

---

[110] Quran, Sūrah al-Baqarah (2), Verse 61:

﴿...مَّا سَأَلْتُمْ ۗ وَضُرِبَتْ عَلَيْهِمُ ٱلذِّلَّةُ وَٱلْمَسْكَنَةُ وَبَآءُو بِغَضَبٍ مِّنَ ٱللَّهِ ۗ...﴿٦١﴾﴾

"...So, in the end, ignominy and misery were pitched upon them, and they earned wrath (a humiliating punishment) from Allah..."

[111] Quran, Sūrah al-Nisā' (4), Verse 46:

﴿مِّنَ ٱلَّذِينَ هَادُوا۟ يُحَرِّفُونَ ٱلْكَلِمَ عَن مَّوَاضِعِهِۦ...﴾

"Among the become Jews are some who alter the words from their context to distort their meanings..."

[112] Quran, Sūrah al-Nisā' (4), Verse 161:

﴿وَأَخْذِهِمُ ٱلرِّبَوٰا۟ وَقَدْ نُهُوا۟ عَنْهُ وَأَكْلِهِمْ أَمْوَٰلَ ٱلنَّاسِ بِٱلْبَٰطِلِ ۚ وَأَعْتَدْنَا لِلْكَٰفِرِينَ مِنْهُمْ عَذَابًا أَلِيمًا ﴿١٦١﴾﴾

"And (because of) their taking interest although it had been forbidden to them, and consuming the wealth of people unjustly (in wrongful ways such as usury, theft, usurpation, bribery, gambling, and disregarding Allah's Revelations); and We have prepared for the disbelievers among them a painful punishment."

to *jihād*: "You and your Lord go and fight; we are sitting here."[113]

Due to these deviations, Allah ﷻ brought them down from the height of honour and virtue to the depths of disgrace and humiliation.

In every prayer, we ask Allah ﷻ not to make us like those who incurred His wrath, meaning not to be among those who distort the verses, engage in usury, or flee from striving on the Path of Truth.

We also ask not to be among those who have gone astray, those who abandon the truth and follow falsehood, who either exaggerate and go to extremes in their beliefs or follow their own desires or the desires of others.[114]

In this chapter, Sūrah al-Fātiḥa, a person expresses their love, devotion, and allegiance to the Prophets, martyrs, and

---

[113] Quran, Sūrah al-Māʾidah (5), Verse 24:

﴿قَالُواْ يَٰمُوسَىٰٓ إِنَّا لَن نَّدۡخُلَهَآ أَبَدٗا مَّا دَامُواْ فِيهَا فَٱذۡهَبۡ أَنتَ وَرَبُّكَ فَقَٰتِلَآ إِنَّا
هَٰهُنَا قَٰعِدُونَ ٢٤﴾

"They said: 'O Mūsā! Indeed, we will never enter it if they are there. Go forth then, you and your Lord, and fight, both of you. (As for ourselves) Indeed, we will just be sitting here!'"

[114] Quran, Sūrah al-Māʾidah (5), Verse 77:

﴿قُلۡ يَٰٓأَهۡلَ ٱلۡكِتَٰبِ لَا تَغۡلُواْ فِي دِينِكُمۡ غَيۡرَ ٱلۡحَقِّ وَلَا تَتَّبِعُوٓاْ أَهۡوَآءَ قَوۡمٖ قَدۡ ضَلُّواْ
مِن قَبۡلُ وَأَضَلُّواْ كَثِيرٗا وَضَلُّواْ عَن سَوَآءِ ٱلسَّبِيلِ ٧٧﴾

"Say: 'O People of the Book! Do not exceed the limits in your religion, (straying towards) other than the truth, and do not follow the lusts and fancies of a people who went astray before, and led many others astray, and they strayed from the right way.'"

righteous individuals, and asks for being kept on the straight path that they adhered to, while also disassociating from and rejecting those who incurred the wrath of Allah ﷻ and the misguided throughout history. This is the embodiment of *tawallī* (loving the virtuous ones and their righteous deeds), and *tabarrī* (disassociating from evil people and their inappropriate actions).

The Misguided in the Quran

The word "misguidance," along with its derivatives, appears around 200 times in the Quran. Sometimes, it is used in the sense of bewilderment: "And He found you lost and guided you;"[115] and other times, it means wasting or losing: "Those who disbelieve and avert (people) from the way of Allah, He will render their deeds to be lost (make them worthless)."[116] However, most often it refers to misguidance, appearing with various descriptions such as "clear misguidance," "far misguidance," and "great misguidance."

The Quran identifies certain individuals as being misguided, including those who exchanged their faith for

---

[115] Quran, Sūrah al-Ḍuḥā (93), Verse 7:

﴿وَوَجَدَكَ ضَآلًّا فَهَدَىٰ ۝٧﴾

[116] Quran, Sūrah Muḥammad (47), Verse 1:

﴿ٱلَّذِينَ كَفَرُوا۟ وَصَدُّوا۟ عَن سَبِيلِ ٱللَّهِ أَضَلَّ أَعْمَـٰلَهُمْ ۝١﴾

"Those who disbelieve and bar (people) from the Way of Allah – He will render all their deeds vain."

disbelief,[117] the polytheists,[118] the disbelievers,[119] the sinners,[120] Muslims who took disbelievers as their

---

[117] Quran, Sūrah al-Baqarah (2), Verse 108:

﴿وَمَن يَتَبَدَّلِ ٱلۡكُفۡرَ بِٱلۡإِيمَٰنِ فَقَدۡ ضَلَّ سَوَآءَ ٱلسَّبِيلِ ١٠٨﴾

"And whoever exchanges faith for disbelief has surely strayed from the right way."

[118] Quran, Sūrah al-Nisāʾ (4), Verse 116:

﴿إِنَّ ٱللَّهَ لَا يَغۡفِرُ أَن يُشۡرَكَ بِهِۦ وَيَغۡفِرُ مَا دُونَ ذَٰلِكَ لِمَن يَشَآءُۚ وَمَن يُشۡرِكۡ بِٱللَّهِ فَقَدۡ ضَلَّ ضَلَٰلَۢا بَعِيدًا ١١٦﴾

"Indeed, Allah does not forgive that partners be associated with Him; less than that He forgives for whomever He Wills. And whoever associates partners with Allah has indeed strayed far away (from the Straight Path)."

[119] Quran, Sūrah al-Nisāʾ (4), Verse 136:

﴿يَٰٓأَيُّهَا ٱلَّذِينَ ءَامَنُوٓاْ ءَامِنُواْ بِٱللَّهِ وَرَسُولِهِۦ وَٱلۡكِتَٰبِ ٱلَّذِي نَزَّلَ عَلَىٰ رَسُولِهِۦ وَٱلۡكِتَٰبِ ٱلَّذِيٓ أَنزَلَ مِن قَبۡلُۚ وَمَن يَكۡفُرۡ بِٱللَّهِ وَمَلَٰٓئِكَتِهِۦ وَكُتُبِهِۦ وَرُسُلِهِۦ وَٱلۡيَوۡمِ ٱلۡأٓخِرِ فَقَدۡ ضَلَّ ضَلَٰلَۢا بَعِيدًا ١٣٦﴾

"O you who believe! Believe in Allah, and His Messenger (Muḥammad), and the Book He has been sending down on His Messenger, and the (Divine) Books which He sent down before. And whoever disbelieves in Allah, and His angels, and His Books, and His Messengers, and the Last Day, has certainly gone far astray."

[120] Quran, Sūrah al-Aḥzāb (33), Verse 36:

﴿وَمَا كَانَ لِمُؤۡمِنٖ وَلَا مُؤۡمِنَةٍ إِذَا قَضَى ٱللَّهُ وَرَسُولُهُۥٓ أَمۡرًا أَن يَكُونَ لَهُمُ ٱلۡخِيَرَةُ مِنۡ أَمۡرِهِمۡۗ وَمَن يَعۡصِ ٱللَّهَ وَرَسُولَهُۥ فَقَدۡ ضَلَّ ضَلَٰلٗا مُّبِينٗا ٣٦﴾

"And when Allah and His Messenger have decreed a matter, it is not for a believing man or a believing woman to have an option protectors and friends,[121] those who prevent others from following the path of Allah ﷻ, those who insult Allah ﷻ or His Messenger, those who conceal the truth, and those who despair of the Mercy of Allah ﷻ.

Additionally, the Quran mentions certain figures as 'misguiders,' such as Iblīs (Satan), Pharaoh, Sāmirī, bad friends and associates, and corrupt leaders and ancestors.

The misguided themselves create the foundation and circumstances for their own deviation, while misguiders exploit these ready conditions. The Quran identifies the following as sources of misguidance:

1. Ones's desires.[122]
2. Idols.[123]

---

insofar as they themselves are concerned. And whoever disobeys Allah and His Messenger has evidently gone astray."

[121] Quran, Sūrah al-Mumtaḥanah (60), Verse 1.

[122] Quran, Sūrah al-Jāthiyah (45), Verse 23:

﴿أَفَرَءَيْتَ مَنِ ٱتَّخَذَ إِلَـٰهَهُۥ هَوَىٰهُ وَأَضَلَّهُ ٱللَّهُ عَلَىٰ عِلْمٍ وَخَتَمَ عَلَىٰ سَمْعِهِۦ وَقَلْبِهِۦ وَجَعَلَ عَلَىٰ بَصَرِهِۦ غِشَـٰوَةً فَمَن يَهْدِيهِ مِنۢ بَعْدِ ٱللَّهِ ۚ أَفَلَا تَذَكَّرُونَ ﴿٢٣﴾﴾

"Have you seen the one who has taken their lusts for their deity, and whom Allah has (consequently) led astray though they have knowledge (of guidance and straying), and He sealed their hearing and their heart, and put a cover over their sight? Who then, can guide them after Allah (has led them astray)? Will you not then reflect and be mindful?"

[123] Quran, Sūrah Ibrāhīm (14), Verse 30:

﴿وَجَعَلُوا۟ لِلَّهِ أَندَادًا لِّيُضِلُّوا۟ عَن سَبِيلِهِۦ ۗ قُلْ تَمَتَّعُوا۟ فَإِنَّ مَصِيرَكُمْ إِلَى ٱلنَّارِ ﴿٣٠﴾﴾

"And they have set up rivals to Allah (as deities, lords, and objects of worship), so they have deviated (themselves and other

3. Sins.[124]
4. Accepting false authority.[125]
5. Ignorance.[126]

---

people) from His way. Say: 'Enjoy yourselves (in this world); for indeed, your destination is the Fire.'"

124 Quran, Sūrah al-Baqarah (2), Verse 26:

﴿إِنَّ ٱللَّهَ لَا يَسْتَحْيِۦٓ أَن يَضْرِبَ مَثَلًا مَّا بَعُوضَةً فَمَا فَوْقَهَا ۚ فَأَمَّا ٱلَّذِينَ ءَامَنُوا۟ فَيَعْلَمُونَ أَنَّهُ ٱلْحَقُّ مِن رَّبِّهِمْ ۖ وَأَمَّا ٱلَّذِينَ كَفَرُوا۟ فَيَقُولُونَ مَاذَآ أَرَادَ ٱللَّهُ بِهَٰذَا مَثَلًا ۘ يُضِلُّ بِهِۦ كَثِيرًا وَيَهْدِى بِهِۦ كَثِيرًا ۚ وَمَا يُضِلُّ بِهِۦٓ إِلَّا ٱلْفَٰسِقِينَ ﴿٢٦﴾﴾

"Indeed, Allah is not timid to present a parable – (that of) something like a gnat (a mosquito) or something even lower than it. And those who have already believed know that it is the truth from their Lord. But as for those who disbelieve, they say: 'What does Allah mean by such a parable?' Thereby, He leads many astray, and thereby He guides many. And He misleads none (astray) except the transgressors."

125 Quran, Sūrah al-Ḥajj (22), Verse 4:

﴿كُتِبَ عَلَيْهِ أَنَّهُۥ مَن تَوَلَّاهُ فَأَنَّهُۥ يُضِلُّهُۥ وَيَهْدِيهِ إِلَىٰ عَذَابِ ٱلسَّعِيرِ ﴿٤﴾﴾

"It is decreed about him (Satan) that whoever takes him for a guardian, surely he will lead them astray, and guide to the punishment of the Blaze."

126 Quran, Sūrah al-Baqarah (2), Verse 198:

﴿لَيْسَ عَلَيْكُمْ جُنَاحٌ أَن تَبْتَغُوا۟ فَضْلًا مِّن رَّبِّكُمْ ۚ فَإِذَآ أَفَضْتُم مِّنْ عَرَفَٰتٍ فَٱذْكُرُوا۟ ٱللَّهَ عِندَ ٱلْمَشْعَرِ ٱلْحَرَامِ ۖ وَٱذْكُرُوهُ كَمَا هَدَىٰكُمْ وَإِن كُنتُم مِّن قَبْلِهِۦ لَمِنَ ٱلضَّآلِّينَ ﴿١٩٨﴾﴾

"There is no blame on you that you should seek from the bounty of your Lord (during *Ḥajj*). When you depart from ʿArafāt, then mention Allah at Mashʿar al-Ḥaram (Muzdalifah); and remember

Those who obey Allah ﷻ and His Messenger will be among those whom Allah ﷻ has blessed—the Prophets, the truthful, the martyrs, and the righteous.[127]

Take Away Messages

1. Human beings need role models in their upbringing. The Prophets, martyrs, the truthful, and the righteous are beautiful examples for all of humanity.
2. What comes from Allah ﷻ to human beings is a blessing. We ourselves create anger and wrath.
3. Expressing aversion to those who have incurred the wrath of Allah ﷻ and the misguided will strengthen the Muslim community against accepting their governance.

Him, as He guided you, for indeed, you were before that among those astray."

[127] Quran, Sūrah al-Nisā' (4), Verse 69:

﴿ وَمَن يُطِعِ ٱللَّهَ وَٱلرَّسُولَ فَأُوْلَٰٓئِكَ مَعَ ٱلَّذِينَ أَنْعَمَ ٱللَّهُ عَلَيْهِم مِّنَ ٱلنَّبِيِّـۧنَ
وَٱلصِّدِّيقِينَ وَٱلشُّهَدَآءِ وَٱلصَّٰلِحِينَ ۚ وَحَسُنَ أُوْلَٰٓئِكَ رَفِيقًا ٦٩ ﴾

"And whoever obeys Allah and the Messenger – those will be with the ones whom Allah has favoured – the Prophets, and the truthful ones, and the witnesses, and the righteous ones. How excellent they are for companions!"

Conclusion by the Translator

Alḥamdulillāh, we have reached the conclusion of the commentary on Sūrah al-Fātiḥa, the opening chapter of the Quran. This chapter, often referred to as the 'Mother of the Book' *(Umm al-Kitāb)*, holds a central place in the daily lives of Muslims, serving as the essence of the Quran's message and a cornerstone of Islamic worship. Throughout this commentary, Shaykh Muḥsin Qarāʾatī endeavoured to illuminate the profound meanings and lessons embedded in this short, yet comprehensive chapter.

Sūrah al-Fātiḥa begins with praise and recognition of Allah's ﷻ Attributes of Mercy and Lordship; and progresses to an acknowledgment of human dependence on Divine guidance. It encapsulates the believer's goal: to remain on The Straight Path *(Ṣirāṭ al-Mustaqīm)* – a path marked by the favour of Allah ﷻ upon His righteous servants, who are free from deviation or misguidance.

Shaykh Qarāʾatī's commentary delved into each verse, unraveling some of the theological, ethical, and practical dimensions of this chapter. He highlighted the importance of recognizing Allah's ﷻ Mercy as foundational to our relationship with Him; the acknowledgment of His Sovereignty over the Day of Judgement, and the exclusive reliance on Him for assistance. Moreover, he draws our attention to the supplicatory nature of this chapter, emphasizing that sincere prayer for guidance should be at the heart of a believer's relationship with Allah ﷻ.

Another key theme explored in this first chapter of the Quran is the collective nature of supplication. By using the plural pronouns "we" and "us" throughout the chapter, the Quran reminds us about the communal aspect of faith. This serves as a reminder that while our spiritual journey is personal, it is also interconnected with the broader community *(ummah)*. Our supplication for guidance is not only for ourselves, but also for our brothers and sisters in faith, reinforcing the bonds of unity and mutual responsibility.

Shaykh also shed light on the contrasts presented in this chapter: The path of those who have earned Allah's ﷻ favour, versus those who have gone astray. This duality serves as a moral compass for believers, encouraging self-reflection and vigilance in maintaining righteousness, while avoiding the pitfalls of arrogance, ignorance, or heedlessness.

Through his commentary, Shaykh Qarā'atī has emphasized that Sūrah al-Fātiḥa is not merely a chapter to be recited in prayer, but a source of ongoing guidance, inspiration, and renewal for a believer. It invites us to ponder the infinite wisdom of Allah ﷻ, and to continuously seek His mercy and guidance in all aspects of our lives. The Shaykh's reflections encourage us to engage with the Quran – not only as a text to be recited, but as a living guide to be understood, internalized, and acted upon.

As we conclude this commentary, it is important to reflect on the responsibility that comes with this understanding. The lessons derived from Sūrah al-Fātiḥa, and the call for action – to embody gratitude, humility, and a constant striving for Divine guidance. They remind us to align our intentions, thoughts, and deeds with the principles of Islam, ensuring that our lives are a testimony to the transformative power of the Quranic message.

With the completion of this commentary on Sūrah al-Fātiḥa, we look forward to the publication of Shaykh Muḥsin Qarā'atī's insights into other chapters of the Quran. The Shaykh's approach – grounded in simplicity, accessibility, and practical relevance – will undoubtedly continue to provide invaluable guidance to readers seeking to deepen their connection with the Quran. Future commentaries will, *Inshā' Allah*, shed light on other chapters, helping us to navigate the vast ocean of Divine Wisdom contained in the Quran.

We pray to Allah, the All-Compassionate, and All-Merciful, to accept this humble effort from us, to forgive any shortcomings, and to allow the teachings of this commentary to resonate deeply in the hearts of its readers. May it serve as a means of drawing closer to Allah ﷻ, understanding His Message, and implementing it in our daily lives.

Other Publications Available[128]

1. *A Land Most Goodly: The Story of Yemen in the Quran and in the Times of Prophet Muḥammad and Imam ʿAlī ibn Abī Ṭālib,* by Jaffer Ladak
2. *A Star Amongst the Stars: The Life and Times of the Great Companion: Jabir ibn Abdullah al-Ansari,* by Jaffer Ladak*
3. *Alif, Baa, Taa of Kerbala,* by Saleem Bhimji and Arifa Hudda
4. *Arbāʿīn of Imam Ḥusayn,* compiled and translated by Saleem Bhimji
5. *Daily Devotions,* compiled and translated by Saleem Bhimji*
6. *Deficient? A Review of Sermon 80 from Nahj al-Balāgha,* by Āyatullāh al-ʿUẓmā Shaykh Nāṣir Makārim Shīrāzī and translated by Saleem Bhimji
7. *Exegesis of the 29th Juz of the Quran a Translation of Tafsīr Nemunah,* by Āyatullāh al-ʿUẓmā Shaykh Nāṣir

[128] The following is a list of all the original writings and translations from the Islamic Publishing House. As many of these titles are out of stock, we are slowly re-releasing all our works via Print-on-Demand through Amazon.

Titles with an * after the name are currently available via Amazon from their international platforms, including Australia, Canada, France, Germany, Italy, Japan, UK, USA, Netherlands, and Spain.

If you cannot find any of the above titles on Amazon, feel free to email us at **iph@iph.ca**.

Makārim Shīrāzī and translated by Saleem Bhimji*

8. *Foundations of Islamic Unity* a translation of *Al-Fuṣūl al-Muhimmah fī Ta'līf al-Ummah,* by ʿAbd al-Ḥusayn Sharaf al-Dīn al-Mūsawī al-ʿĀmilī and translated by Batool Ispahany*
9. *Fountain of Paradise: Fāṭima az-Zahrā' in the Noble Quran,* by Āyatullāh al-ʿUẓmā Shaykh Nāṣir Makārim Shīrāzī, compiled and translated by Saleem Bhimji*
10. *God and god of Science,* by Syed Hasan Raza Jafri*
11. *House of Sorrows,* by Shaykh ʿAbbās al-Qummī and translated by Aejaz Ali Turab Husayn Husayni*
12. *Iʿtikāf: The Spiritual Retreat – The Philosophy, Spiritual Mysteries and Practical Rulings,* compiled and translated by Saleem Bhimji*
13. *Inspirational Insights,* by Mohammed Khaku
14. *Islam and Religious Pluralism,* by Āyatullāh Shaykh Murtaḍā Muṭahharī and translated by Sayyid Sulayman Ali Hasan
15. *Journey to Eternity – A Handbook of Supplications for the Soul,* compiled and translated by Saleem Bhimji and Arifa Hudda*
16. *Love and Hate for Allah's Sake,* by Mujtaba Saburi translated by Saleem Bhimji
17. *Love for the Family,* compiled and translated by Yasin T. Al-Jibouri, Saleem Bhimji, and others*
18. *Moral Management,* by Abbas Rahimi and translated by Saleem Bhimji*
19. *Morals of the Masumeen,* by Arifa Hudda
20. *Prayers of the Final Prophet – A Collection of Supplications of Prophet Muḥammad,* by ʿAllāmah Sayyid Muḥammad Ḥusayn Ṭabā'ṭabā'ī and translated

by Tahir Ridha-Jaffer*

21. *Prospering Through a Cost of Living Crisis*, by Jaffer Ladak*
22. *Ramaḍān Reflections*, compiled by A Group of Muslim Scholars and translated by Saleem Bhimji*
23. *Ṣalāt al-Āyāt*, by Saleem Bhimji
24. *Ṣalāt al-Ghufaylah: Salvation through Patience & Perseverance*, written by Saleem Bhimji*
25. *Secrets of the Ḥajj*, by Āyatullāh al-ʿUẓmā Shaykh Ḥusayn Mazāherī and translated by Saleem Bhimji
26. *Sunan an-Nabī*, by ʿAllāmah Sayyid Muḥammad Ḥusayn Ṭabāʾṭabāʾī and translated by Tahir Ridha-Jaffer
27. *Tears from Heaven's Flowers: An Anthology of English Poetry about the Ahlulbayt*, by Abrahim al-Zubeidi
28. *The Day the Germs Caused Fitnah*, by Umm Maryam*
29. *The Firmest Armament: Commentary on Āyatul Kursī (The Verse of the Throne)*, by Sayyid Nasrullah Burujerdi and translated by Saleem Bhimji*
30. *The Last Luminary and Ways to Delve into the Light*, by Sayyid Muḥammad Ridha Husayni Mutlaq and translated by Saleem Bhimji*
31. *The Muslim Legal Will Booklet*, by Saleem Bhimji*
32. *The Pure Life*, by Āyatullāh al-ʿUẓmā as-Sayyid Muḥammad Taqī al-Modarresī and translated by Jaffer Ladak with commentary by Dr. Zainali Panjwani and Jaffer Ladak*
33. *The Third Testimony: Imam ʿAlī in the Adhān*, compiled and translated by Saleem Bhimji*
34. *The Tragedy of Kerbalāʾ*, as narrated by Imam ʿAlī ibn al-Ḥusayn al-Sajjād ﷺ, recorded by Shaykh al-Ṣadūq and translated by ʿAbdul Zahrāʾ ʿAbdul Ḥusayn*

35. *The Torch of Perpetual Guidance – A Brief Commentary on Ziyārat al-ʿĀshūrā'*, by ʿAbbās Azizi and translated by Saleem Bhimji
36. *Weapon of the Believer,* by ʿAllāmah Muḥammad Bāqir Majlisī and translated by Saleem Bhimji*

Upcoming Publications

1. *Beyond the 40th: Understanding the Exclusive Significance of the Arbaʿīn of Imam al-Ḥusayn*, by the late Āyatullāh al-Sayyid Muḥammad Muḥsin Ḥusaynī Ṭehrānī, translated by Saleem Bhimji
2. *Guided By Faith: The Islamic Management Model,* written by ʿAbbās Raḥīmī, translated by Saleem Bhimji
3. *Knocking on Heaven's Doors*, compiled with translations by Saleem Bhimji
4. *Propaganda and Piety: The Umayyad Rewriting of Syria [From Historical Syria to Apocalyptic Syria]*, written by Dr. Rasūl Jaʿfariyān, translated by Saleem Bhimji
5. *Ramaḍān Devotions: A Collection of Supplications for the Nights of Qadr*, compiled with translations by Saleem Bhimji
6. *Blessed Desires: Islamic Perspectives on Sexuality and the Soul*, by ʿAlī Ḥoseinzādeh, translated by Saleem Bhimji
7. *Shadows of Dissent*, by Āyatullāh Shaykh Nāṣir Makārim Shīrāzī, translated by Saleem Bhimji and the Translator's Guild of the Islamic Publishing House
8. *Supplication for the People of the Frontiers*, by Shaykh Ḥusayn Anṣāriān, translated by Saleem Bhimji
9. *The Arbaʿīn: A look into the Ziyārat of Arbaʿīn*, written by Saleem Bhimji
10. *The Comprehensive Book of Marriage and Divorce Formulas*, by Saleem Bhimji
11. *The Young Muslims Daily Devotions Manuals – Volumes I and II*, compiled and translated by Saleem Bhimji

12. *Victor Not Victim: A Biography of Lady Zaynab binte ʿAlī and 200 Short Stories*, researched and written by Saleem Bhimji
13. *Weekly Spiritual Ascent: Ṣalāt al-Jumuʿah: Philosophy, Practice, and Personal Piety*, compiled and translated by Saleem Bhimji

Our *Living the Quran Through The Living Quran* series of commentary on the Noble Quran is also being published. To date, we have released the commentary of:

1. Sūrah al-Fātiḥa (1)
2. Sūrah Yāsīn (36)
3. Sūrah Qāf (50)
4. Sūrah al-Najm (53)
5. Sūrah al-Wāqiʿah (56)
6. Sūrah al-Mujādilah (58)

The commentary of the following chapters of the Quran will also be released in the future:

1. Sūrah al-Ṣaff (61)

Supporting Our Projects

If you would like to donate to any of our ongoing projects, such as our upcoming book publications, video content, or articles, you can contribute in the following ways:

Within Canada: Send an e-transfer from your Canadian bank account to **iph@iph.ca**

International: Send your transfer via PayPal to **saleem1176@rogers.com**

For more information,
check out our website:

www.iph.ca

Contact us for more information at:

iph@iph.ca

www.ingramcontent.com/pod-product-compliance
Lightning Source LLC
Chambersburg PA
CBHW032019040426
42448CB00006B/673
* 9 7 8 1 9 2 7 9 3 0 6 3 2 *